Percy Russell

A Guide to British and American Novels

Percy Russell

A Guide to British and American Novels

ISBN/EAN: 9783744760805

Printed in Europe, USA, Canada, Australia, Japan

Cover: Foto ©Thomas Meinert / pixelio.de

More available books at **www.hansebooks.com**

A GUIDE

TO

BRITISH AND AMERICAN NOVELS

BEING A COMPREHENSIVE MANUAL OF ALL FORMS
OF POPULAR FICTION IN GREAT BRITAIN,
AUSTRALASIA, AND AMERICA FROM
ITS COMMENCEMENT DOWN
TO 1894

BY

PERCY RUSSELL

AUTHOR OF "THE AUTHORS' MANUAL," "A JOURNEY TO LAKE TAUPO;
AUSTRALIAN TALES," ETC.

SECOND EDITION, CAREFULLY REVISED

LONDON

DIGBY, LONG & CO., PUBLISHERS

18 BOUVERIE STREET, FLEET STREET, E.C.

1895

CONTENTS

PREFACE

THIS book is the result of thirty-six years continuous study of British, American, and Australasian fiction.

Obviously few general readers in these busy days have leisure to read the novels of the past; and yet some knowledge of these is important, while, through ignorance of how to select judiciously amid the myriads of old or comparatively old novels and romances, the contemporary reader is sorely perplexed and inevitably deprived of very much pleasure and profit, through want of the necessary guide.

The object of this manual is to place before readers, in succinct form, a trustworthy account, brief as is compatible with lucidity, of most of the principal novels and romances of the past. Readers can select thence whatever appears most suited to their tastes, or remain content with the information here given. That information is expressly designed to be adequate for all who desire to be well informed on the salient features and as to all the masterpieces in every department of British prose fiction at home and over the seas, from its very beginning until the present day.

In a word, the possession of this Guide will, it is hoped, make the reader at least sufficiently acquainted with all the great or noteworthy fiction of the past, and thus liberate each reader's available leisure for perusing the fiction of the present, which is now pouring in upon us in such a volume, as to leave for those who follow its courses little if any opportunity to become acquainted directly even with the best of that which forms the standard fiction of the past.

To fully meet this pressing and ever-increasing need, by enabling even those with least leisure to become practically conversant with the epochs and masterpieces of British fiction during more than two centuries, is the object and purpose of this Guide.

P. R.

June, 1894.

PREFACE TO THE SECOND
EDITION

ALTHOUGH this book was issued quite recently, a new edition is already necessary. I take, therefore, this opportunity of expressing my thanks to those discerning reviewers who have been good enough to indicate some errors and omissions in a work which, from its very character and extensive scope, was especially liable to such defects. While, however, frankly acknowledging my indebtedness to those who have thus aided to improve a book designed to bring an outline history of British fiction into a convenient compendium, I cannot refrain from referring to certain critics who have succeeded, to their own satisfaction, in "discovering" "errors" which do not exist, and who evidently think that the main aim of reviewing is to misrepresent, and to substitute for criticism mere assumption and prejudice. Thus, one very positive reviewer accuses me of omitting re-

PREFACE TO THE SECOND EDITION.

ference to the tales, etc., of Mr. Rudyard
Kipling precedent to the publication of *The
Light that Failed.* Yet a glance at page
230 will show that I *have* referred to the
tales. Another reviewer discovers that the
name of Le Fanu, the well-known novelist,
is not mentioned in the Index to Authors;
yet the name is there notwithstanding. Then
again, while one reviewer pronounces my
method of arrangement to be good, another
declares that it is very bad! Finally, I am
blamed for not including Cervantes among
British and American novelists! In conclusion, I must convey my warm thanks to many
readers in all quarters, for their general ap-
proval of the plan and execution of a work,
which, whatever may be its shortcomings,
still fills what was previously a gap in our
reference literature.

P. R.

January, 1895.

INTRODUCTORY

IT has been aptly said that a taste for reading is in itself a true agency for obtaining real happiness, and that essential constituent of happiness—contentment. But in the face of the multitude of books, past and present, and of those continually pouring forth from the press, the question—*What shall I read?* is becoming equally pressing and serious to all of us, whether we read as students, as connoisseurs, or simply for recreative purposes. Very obviously we cannot read *all* the books, either past or present; and in selecting works that are not of the best we lose much, while we lose still more in selecting those that are bad or false, or in any way unworthy to be called literature. Then, moreover, we are faced with the increased difficulty that, just as books are multiplying with astounding rapidity, so does the leisure of most of us contract, owing to the press and hurry of competitive life; and thus, more than ever, is it important to read wisely and well.

It is not, of course, possible for many of us at

any period in our lives to give very much solid time to general literature; and few, indeed, can truly say, with the poet Southey—

> My days among the dead are passed;
> Around me I behold,
> Where'er these casual eyes are cast,
> The mighty minds of old.

And, then, there are books in increasing numbers now which are, for the most part, but the diluted reproductions of already existing standard works, which should, indeed, be read in preference to the mere book-making replicas, or copies. Just as maps are essential to aid the traveller to find his way in unknown regions, so, it seems to me, is an intelligent, and, of course, impartial guide essential in these times of books without end, to help the reader to the best among them, and to enable him or her to read to true profit, and in such a way as to really obtain culture, which should always be one direct issue of reading generally.

There is also the question of quality before quantity. Haste is one of the worst characteristics of our time; and railway speed in reading leads to neither profit nor pleasure in the end, but often eventually results in a rooted distaste to any solid reading, and induces a vicious appetite for what may be called the confectionery side of amusing literature—for scraps, anecdotes, jokes, and sensations, which, all very well in their due place, become, when taken *en masse*, ruinous to the mental digestion for all that is really lofty and good, and of permanent gain to the careful reader. In these days too many devote themselves mainly to skimming what they erroneously consider the cream of literature, but what is more often merely its rhetorical froth, devoid of substance and of real worth; and then, in addition to this, many read so idly that little or no impression is produced on their minds, and they become, in one word, mentally impervious. A good book, carefully read and thought over, does more in the way of cultivating the reader's mind than a library of circulating fiction of the ordinary kind, and it will also help to furnish the memory with unfailing and often rich resources against the tedium of hours when that memory is driven to feed on its own resources.

In *Never Too Late to Mend* we are told of the prison chaplain who experimented himself on the horrors of solitary confinement in the dark; and he declares that, but for his resources of memory from reading, he could not have borne the infliction, which must, therefore, he argues rightly enough, have been an unjustifiably cruel torture for those who had no mental resources of their own. It is, then, to reading, to a great extent, that we should

look for the furnishing of our mind against the
future; and every book read is decidedly a gain or
loss mentally.

Thus it will be readily admitted that guidance
of some kind is all-important in this matter, and
the more so when we consider what a world of
books there is. Poetry, fiction, science, history,
biography, and much more, are before us; and
truly it is bewildering at first to contemplate
this world of books, and to know that in *some*, but
surely not in all, or even in very many, perhaps,
there are mighty ethical forces, true spiritual
powers, to rouse, educate, and develop our souls,
if only we can chance to come on the right books.
In the following chapters I take the novels of the
past in detail under their respective phases and
divisions; but, as a preliminary, it is well to inquire
briefly into the beginnings of prose fiction generally,
and to glance at the original germs of the novel as
we now know it.

CHAPTER I.

A BRIEF SKETCH OF THE ORIGIN AND DEVELOPMENT OF THE NOVEL.

THE novel has now expanded to the dimensions of a literature, and, after the slow evolution of over two centuries, has, at last, come to the very forefront as one of the greatest intellectual forces of the age. Whatever now greatly moves or interests society soon finds its vehicle in some form of fiction; and thus, curiously enough, the novel is more than ever faithful to its Italian name, *novella, i.e., news.*

But if we go down to the roots of prose fiction, we must glance back not two centuries, but more than 2000 years. The remote origin of the novel, which a living novelist has aptly called "a pocket play," lies certainly in the ancient drama; and, after all, a good work of fiction is practically a portable theatre, containing, as it does, within its covers, scenery, actors, actresses, dialogues, and all the charming paraphernalia to the mind's eye, to the vision of the imagination, that renders the theatre so fascinating; and all this, too, minus the dis-

I

advantages that attend thereon. The novelist, moreover, is the domestic annalist, and the chosen exponent of life in all its kaleidoscopic phases. He is the universal cicerone to all places; he introduces us to all human types, he holds up the mirror to nature, and reports for our delectation the sayings of men, women, and children, wherein we are most interested, laying bare the human heart, and diving down into the infinite complexities of human motive.

The very roots of the novel carry us back, indeed, to the youth of the world; for the earliest examples of prose fiction are generally allowed to be the *Milesian Tales* of Aristides. The Milesians were Ionic Greeks; and one of the latest labours of the first Lord Lytton was a translation of some supposed fragments that have survived of these tales.

Probably the germ of the true novel lies in the invention of Arab story-tellers; and thus the novel, like so many more of our intellectual gains, has come to us from the Orient. Lucian, the well-known Greek satirist (2nd century), was a story-teller; Heliodorus (4th century), wrote the history of two lovers—*Chariclea and Theagenes;* but doubtless a better known work is the *Golden Ass* of Apuleius, wherein are narrated the surprising adventures of a young man changed into an ass. Thence, indeed, Boccaccio drew material; and he, in his turn, was laid under contribution by Le Sage (born 1668), in *Gil Blas*.

With the break-up of the Roman Empire and the complete establishment of feudalism in Europe, there came a great wave of extravagant and often unnatural romance, wherein are woven together the wild myths of the old Keltic races, the classic types of ancient Rome, and a tincture of the fantasy and occasionally the wild and wonderful things of the East, derived through the medium of the crusades. Thus history, myth, poetry, and fable were blended together, and the fifteenth century witnessed the birth of the extravagant fiction of Raoul Le Febre, who is accredited with the romance of *Medea and Jason*. Jason is a "knight," and the whole conception is an absurd medley of Western chivalry and Greek mythology.

It is not my purpose to go into the details of this indeterminate period in the gradual evolution of the novel as we have it now. Few, if any, of the elaborate romances like *Amadis de Gaul* (1485),*Huon of Bordeaux*, which, however, suggested the opera *Oberon*, or even the famous *Legenda Aurea*, would have any real interest for the modern reader. It was not until the sixteenth century, if indeed so early, that fiction, as we understand it, began to crystal- lise into an approximation to the modern novel, presenting, rather curiously, many of the now

familiar types. In the ancient forms of what may
be called the classic embryo of the modern novel,
there are usually certain features which, modified
by circumstance, run through all works of this
type. The hero, and especially the heroine, are
invariably the objective points of plot, treachery,
and persecution; and the whole art of the narrator
is usually exerted to separate hero and heroine,
who are only united at the close. Every kind of
material agency is invoked, and the supernatural
has here ample scope, thus curiously enough antici-
pating the occult novel of the nineteenth century.
There was a great vogue for such stories in the
earlier period of the Christian era, and many of the
romances current seem to have grown as writer
after writer took up stock themes and elaborated
them beyond his predecessors. In the satiric
tales of Rabelais (1495-1553), we have surely an
intimation of that comic and humorous fiction
which culminates in *Pickwick* and in "Mark Twain"
(Mr. Samuel L. Clemens).

Sir Thomas More gives in his *Utopia* (1480-
1535) probably the earliest form of the political
romance or novel, as Sir Philip Sidney (1554-1586)
in *Arcadia* gave us the pastoral novel, while
Thomas Lodge (1556-1625), in his romance
Rosalynde, furnished, it is generally believed,
much material for Shakespeare's *As You Like It.*

The Elizabethan period was very barren in prose fiction ; but if we may consider the play to be the novel in action, then, indeed, we find on the stage much of what was to be the source of inspiration for some of .the great novelists to come.   It is not until we arrive at the eighteenth century that we find the true originals of the English novel as we have it now ; and in Defoe (1661-1731) we must acknowledge the real father of British fiction.   The author of *Robinson Crusoe*, the original type of innumerable stories since, wrote the *Adventures of Captain Singleton*, an embryo of the military novel, to follow, and *Colonel Jack*, which has been imitated by George Augustus Sala in his *Captain Dangerous*.   In both, the struggles of a deserted boy against very adverse circumstances supplies the *motif*.   To Defoe, a plain, vigorous and vivid story-teller, a master of realism, before the word was used in its present sense, succeeded Samuel Richardson (1687-1761), a sentimental, tedious, but exact narrator, who gave in *Sir Charles Grandison*, however, a clear portrait of an ideal gentleman, the faint foreshadowing of Thackeray's fine and finished conception, Colonel Newcome, in that well-known novel the *Newcomes*.   Fielding (1707-1754) followed.   He was a robust contrast to the somewhat puling sentimentality of Richardson, the author of *Clarissa Harlowe*, whose special

representative work is *Pamela ;* and curiously as
we look back on these two romances, we see in
them a dim anticipation of novels like the *Ernest
Maltravers* of the first Lord Lytton. With this
period the novel began to be more generally ap-
preciated. Smollett (1721-1771) was a coarse
anticipator of Captain Marryat (1792-1848) ; while
Sterne (1713-1768), in the *Sentimental Journey* and
in *Tristram Shandy,* showed the way to the more
metaphysical or moralising school of novels. A
little later, Goldsmith (1728-1774), in his one novel,
the *Vicar of Wakefield,* demonstrated what could be
done in the pure domestic and idyllic vein. The
next phase was a powerful outburst of the historic
spirit in novel-writing; and in 1769 Horace Walpole
may be said to have really initiated the romantic
historic type of novel with the *Castle of Otranto.*
Clara Reeve (1725-1803) improved on this with
the *Old English Baron,* and in a sense prepared the
way for Mrs. Anne Radcliffe (1764-1823), who
wrote the *Romance of the Forest,* the *Mysteries of
Udolpho,* the *Italian,* etc. These works abound with
laboured delineations of external nature, and revel
in scenes of feudal pomp, while gloom and terror
are ever present. Imprisoned maidens and splendid but unprincipled cavaliers and diabolical
villains are among the leading characters. To
Mrs. Radcliffe succeeded Matthew Gregory Lewis

(1775-1818), author of the *Monk*, a novel of passion and terror; while Charles Maturin (1782-1824) produced several fantastic romances, the *Fatal Revenge* being a type.

In these novels we find a superabundance of startling incidents, often beyond the range of probability; while cruel noblemen, bandits, old castles, haunted rooms, phantoms and terrible crimes, are among the principal agencies employed to produce an effect. In one word, we have in these works very much that is exaggerated and more or less false to nature and ordinary human life and circumstance.

During the transition period from the eighteenth to the nineteenth century there arose a few notable novelists who cannot well be classed under any particular head. But of these, two or three were in a measure the forerunners of great schools that have now reached an extraordinary development. Thus there was Dr. John Moore (1730-1802), who wrote *Zeluco*, a novel in two volumes, wherein the principal character is so atrocious as to excite only horror. William Godwin (1756-1836) deserves special notice, being the author of what has been sometimes called the first English sensational novel, *Caleb Williams* (1794), wherein the severities of our criminal law at that period are duly set forth. Godwin wrote also *St. Leon*, a fine romance, turning on the possession by a mysterious character of an elixir of life; and here we have the further development of an idea, which may be traced in a sequence through *Zanoni* and *A Strange Story*, by the first Lord Lytton, down to the *She* of Mr. Rider Haggard. Madame D'Arblay (1752-1840) must not be forgotten. She was the daughter of Charles Burney, the author of the *History of Music*, and in 1793 married a French emigrant artillery officer. With the restoration of the Bourbons she went to France, but subsequently settled at Bath, where her husband died in 1818. Madame D'Arblay, or Frances Burney, as she was more familiarly known, rose at one period to very considerable literary celebrity as a lady novelist. She produced four principal novels, *Evelina, Cecilia, Camilla,* and the *Wanderer;* the first now alone survives as a memory. It is essentially what it is described as being in the sub-title, namely, the history of a young lady's entrance into the world; and it traces out her career until, at last, she marries a lord, which satisfies her ambition. It is worthy of note, that prior to her marriage, Miss Burney was second keeper of the robes to Queen Charlotte, and she had better opportunities of painting accurately the times among the higher classes than many of her successors at a far later period. *Evelina* was one of the first novels written by a woman, and purporting to be a true picture of life and manners, that is really of sterling merit; and as such it was proclaimed by Lord Macaulay in 1843 in an essay in the *Edinburgh Review*. Miss Burney deserves to be remembered as in some respects the pioneer of the Englishwoman in fiction.

Mary Russell Mitford (1789-1855) wrote some distinctive prose fiction, of which *Atherton*, a three-volume novel, is well-nigh forgotten. It is mainly on account of *Our Village*, sketches of English country life, that she survives in literature. Like Miss L. E. Landon, who also produced some prose fiction, Miss Mitford was more of the poet than the novelist.

Charlotte Brontë (1816-1855) is mainly known as the writer of *Jane Eyre*, a novel which, when it appeared in 1847, achieved an immediate and an extraordinary success. *Jane Eyre* will be found fully dealt with under the section devoted to " Popular Novels of the Past ".

Mrs. Elizabeth Gaskell (1810-1865) began her career in fiction with *Mary Barton* in 1848; and five years later she published *Ruth*. These two novels have special value as delineating the manners, customs, habits and thoughts of the working poor; and their relations to capitalists are powerfully drawn. Indeed, ere the word "realistic" was applied as it now is to a certain class of fiction, Mrs. Gaskell had in a manner shown the way.

Mrs. Inchbald (1753-1821), in her novel *A Simple Story*, initiated a school of mild fiction; and then in Miss Jane Austen (1775-1817) there appeared a distinctly new influence in British fiction. Her novels, *Pride and Prejudice, Sense and Sensibility, Northanger Abbey*, and some others, broke up fresh ground, and portrayed with great truth the everyday life of the middle classes of her times. Miss Austen has an exquisite touch, investing even the commonplace with charms of its own.

In Miss Maria Edgeworth (1761-1849) we have the cause, through her Irish life novels, which is said to have impelled Scott himself to put forth his matchless powers in delineating Scottish character. This naturally brings us to Scott himself, who for the first time painted in wondrous words the grandeur, the majesty, and might of the past, and, what none had done before, gave us much of its mirth and everyday life, to say nothing of its pageantry, which glows so brightly in his pages, and throbs to the full heat of the heroic muse.

Elizabeth Mary Sewell, born about 1812, is another example of the domestic life novelist. It is true that many of her tales are of the kind known as designed for the young; but nevertheless some of them are novels of a high order of merit, and for their moral tone they deserve emphatic praise. Among her works may be cited *Amy Herbert*, *Gertrude*, *The Earl's Daughter*, *Ursula*, *Ivors*, *The Two Cousins*, and *Katherine Ashton*. The most commendable thing about these stories is their high moral tone and the spirit of reverence for all things good and sacred, whereby they are uniformly inspired.

Prior to the epoch of the Waverley novels, however, one work of real genius marks the close of the eighteenth century. This is the *Vathek* of William Beckford (1760-1844), published in 1787. It is an oriental story of great power, especially in one scene, reproducing the supposed hall of Eblis.

G. P. R. James (1801-1860) had a long reign as an historical novelist; and greater far than he was Sir Edward Bulwer (1805-1873), afterwards Lord Lytton; and of his works ample mention is made under other heads. Theodore Hook (1788-1841) in a manner prepared the way with his fun and frolic, as in *Gilbert Gurney* and *Jack Brag*, for the more effective caricature, the delicate fancy and the rich humour of Dickens.

Before passing further, it is in place to mention here a fact not, perhaps, generally known in connection with the early days of Dickens. It is an incident, indeed, which reminds us how small an initial incident may, and often does, determine

the whole drift of a career. Can we imagine how
it would have been with Charles Dickens had his
career as a novelist been postponed, as was
Thackeray's, and had he commenced his career
minus the *Pickwick Papers* ? Yet it was only by the
merest accident that Dickens produced *Pickwick*.
In an interesting volume entitled *A Forgotten
Genius: Charles Whitehead*, by Mackenzie Bell,
we are told that in 1836 Charles Whitehead was
acting as the editor of a library of fiction, and in
this connection arose his intimacy with Charles
Dickens, then a young writer producing his earliest
work. Whitehead was asked to associate himself
with Seymour in producing the book which was
destined to become so famous as the *Pickwick
Papers*. It appears that when Messrs. Chapman
& Hall offered to Whitehead the commission to
write to Seymour's sketches, he declined, on the
ground that he was not equal to the task of producing the copy with sufficient regularity; and he
then, as Mr. Bell informs us, recommended to the
publishers the young author of the *Sketches by Boz*.
This, as we all know, formed the turning-point in
the literary life of Dickens; but had Whitehead
executed the commission to write to Seymour's
sketches himself, as he might so easily have done,
it is curious to speculate how very different
might have been the future development of Dickens,

had his advent as a novelist been postponed, as it would have been but for Whitehead's kindness, a few years longer.

Harrison Ainsworth (1805-1882) was chief of a literary clique known as the Newgate novelists, the heroes of many of his works being highwaymen, desperadoes, murderers, etc. We now come to a host of novelists who are dealt with in detail under the various sections of this book. Charles Dickens (1812-1870) and Thackeray (1811-1863) were contemporary; and then we have Marryat (1792-1848), Charles Lever (1806-1872), Charles and Henry Kingsley (1819-1875, 1830-1876), Lord Beaconsfield (1805-1881); and while throughout much of this period the genius of Charles Dickens was blazing sunlike in the midst of many bright particular stars, there arose the school of avowedly sensational novelists (see separate section), Wilkie Collins (1824-1889) striking the keynote very decidedly with the *Woman in White* (1860); and, in a different degree, Miss Braddon (1837) with *Lady Audley's Secret* in 1862.

Many other names occur. Going backward we find Mrs. Gore (1800-1861), writer of novels relating essentially to fashionable life; Mrs. Norton (1808-1877), Miss Muloch, subsequently Mrs. Craik (1826-1887), authoress of *John Halifax, Gentleman*, and many other novels; Mrs. Oliphant

(1828), Mrs. Riddell (1837), Miss Rhoda Broughton (1840) ; "Ouida," Louise de la Ramée (1840),
and very many more, not forgetting the Brontë
sisters, fully dealt with elsewhere. Then, too, we
have Charles Reade (1814-1884), a writer of vast
power, George Macdonald (1824), Whyte Melville
(1821-1878), R. D. Blackmore, the author of *Lorna
Doone* (1825), William Black (1841), and then was
there not Anthony Trollope (1815-1882), who himself
wrote a small library of novels ? Among the leading
novelists of the day besides those already cited are
Hall Caine (1853), David Christie Murray (1847),
Thomas Hardy (1840), George Meredith (1828),
Walter Besant (1838), James Payn (1830), B. L.
Farjeon (1830), Lucas Malet [Mrs. Harrison], Rider
Haggard (1856), Robert Louis Stevenson[1] (1850),
Mrs. Mona Caird, Mrs. Humphry Ward (1851),
the Earl of Desart, Margaret L. Woods, Miss
Annie Holdsworth, Mr. Frank Harris, Henry Seton
Merriman, Mrs. S. Batson, Clara Lemore, Emily
Dunham, Mrs. Russell Barrington, Mr. J. A.
Steuart, and many others of whom some account
will be found under the sections to which their work
belongs.

As to Australian and American novels generally,
these will be found under separate sections.

[1] Mr. Stevenson died at his residence in Samoa in
December 1894.

Chapter II

A SUGGESTED HISTORICAL COURSE
OF NOVEL READING.

Some system in recreative reading is requisite if the best results are to be secured in the way of enjoyment. This system can be based only on a good general outline sketch of imaginative literature, such as I now propose to give. It will not do to simply read on the bare recommendation of a clerk at a subscription library, or only to take up the book most talked about at the club, or most noticed in the daily papers. It will not be well to read only the books of the day; in literature, of all things, catholicity of taste is essential, if true culture and enjoyment are to result. Those who read only in a narrow groove can have little idea of how much they lose thereby. Reading should be varied as much as diet, and suited to the prevailing mood. There is the season for humour and wit, for fun and frolic, when *Pickwick*, for example, can be thoroughly enjoyed; or when we can fully sympathise with the rollicking, care-defying, lucky

Irishmen of Charles Lever, or the dry drolleries of
Mark Twain.   Horace, with his usual applicability
to all times, says,—

Dulce est desipere in loco ;

or, as it may be freely Englished,—

How pleasant is the seasonable jest !

And the fun that hugs you, and, whether you will
or no, shakes out happy laughter, is often the best
of mental medicines, and of bodily too.

Then there is the higher use of fiction, or recreative reading; for, to those who have an æsthetic
taste, how much may be learned of the world, and
of human life, which, but for the magic of the
novel, would to them remain utterly unknown !

Cribbed, cabined, and confined, as some of us
are by circumstance, it is through the agency of
fiction alone that we can obtain glimpses of
broader, deeper, and fuller lives than our own.
Then, how many of us never step on aught but
pavement or carpet or the smooth-shaven lawn ?
And to such it is no small boon that by just opening a book they can be transported to other ages,
and can revel in scenes that are, to their own environment, as a sunbeam to a straw.   High-toned
fiction, too, is a corrective of much of the bad
influences of contemporary civilisation in its
materialism.   What comfort may not the pessimist

find on turning to the breezy pages of Scott ? Can we not, after drinking deeply of high-class fiction, fraught with pure sentiment and true heroism, exclaim, with Motherwell, that little-known but vigorous north-country lyrist,—

> Let piping swayne and craven wight
>   Still weep, and puling cry,
> *Our* business is like men to fight,
>   And hero-like to die !

Or, again, suppose we have been under the influence of pessimistic or sceptical fiction, shall we stop and look *only* through the intellectual peep-holes furnished by these writers, be they never so gifted ? Surely not. Let us turn, say, to a novel by the author of *John Halifax, Gentleman*, and gain thence quite a new tone of feeling. There, indeed, instead of blighted lives, of doubt-tortured souls or hearths pale with the grey ashes of burned-out domestic love, we shall have glimpses of typical, true English homes, where—

> Gladsome looks of household love
>   Meet in the ruddy light,
> When woman's voice breaks forth in song,
>   Or childhood's tale is told ;
> While lips move tunefully along
>   Some glorious page of old.

Then there are certain subjects in fiction wherein a course of novels in a pre-arranged sequence may

2

be fully equivalent to a regular course of academical lectures,—and how inexpressibly more delightful !

Take history for example. A very complete acquaintance with it, in both its ancient and modern phases, may be obtained from reading a certain selection of novels.

Let us commence, say, with the late Major Whyte Melville's *Sarchedon*, which conveys in a very realistic way the state of ancient Assyrian and Egyptian civilisation, and practically takes up the story of the human race as we find it concluded in the Biblical history of the Hebrew theocracy prior to the choosing of a king.

The rise of Christianity will be found sketched pretty fully in the first Lord Lytton's *Last Days of Pompeii;* while by taking Whyte Melville's *Gladia-tors* (wherein the early Christians again appear), Wilkie Collins' *Antonina*, and *Attila* by G. P. R. James (all in all, perhaps, the best and most finished of his many historical novels), we pass over the decline and fall of the Roman Empire, taking Lord Lytton's *Pausanias* for Greece. It will be perceived that only half a dozen novels here give us a course of ancient history abounding in finely-portrayed, and more or less correctly-costumed, historical personages, and including, as in the battle of Châlons, some of the epochal events in the world's annals.

The perusal of *Harold*, Lord Lytton's finest historical novel, gives us, in fascinating form, not only the Norman Conquest, but the causes leading thereto; and, moreover, it shows us effectively the root differences between Saxon and Norman, and abounds in a fund of antiquities, thoroughly popularised. Sir Walter Scott's *Ivanhoe* introduces us to the Plantagenet period, and shows the origin of the future people of England; while in G. P. R. James'· *Forest Days* we get Henry III., the great Earl Simon de Montford, the battle of Evesham, and the rising splendour of Edward I. *Agincourt*, by the same novelist, as its title suggests, deals with Henry V. and the conquest of France. In Scott's *Quentin Durward* we have Louis XI. and his crooked policy, the beginning of the triumph of the French Crown over the nobles; and in the late Lord Lytton's *Last of the Barons* we have a true chronicle of the first rise to power of the middle and trading classes in England, and the approaching Tudor times. In *Leila, or the Siege of Granada*, by the same writer, we have a full account of the overthrow of the Moors in Spain, and the rise of the great Spanish dominion, to culminate in Charles V.; while *Rienzi*, another of Lord Lytton's romances, serves to explain the complicated political affairs of feudal Italy, and to show the relations of Rome as a temporal power to Europe generally.

If we desire to obtain a thorough insight into
the domestic habits, customs, and manners of the
people of Europe from the Low Countries, through
Germany, and Italy itself, we need only turn to
Charles Reade's finest novel, *The Cloister and the
Hearth,* wherein, moreover, we shall learn the
relations in those days of the priesthood to the
laity, and obtain a very accurate notion of the
tone of public opinion and sentiments in mediæval
Europe.

It is of interest to mention that Charles Reade's
family traces its origin to Tudor times, and the
illustrious novelist claimed descent from Henry
III., thus carrying his ancestry back to a very
remote period. It has been aptly said that in the
blood of Charles Reade was mixed that of mon-
archs and diplomatists, of Calvinists and cavaliers;
and thus, so far as heredity went, this remarkable
novelist combined in himself many ancestral strains
which doubtless veined and worked out his genius
in many ways. It is curious, too, that in boyhood
he was providentially saved from certain death by
being dragged out of Staines church only a second
before the roof tumbled in, the result of "restoration" attempted without shutting up the church.
Reade went to Oxford and was called to the Bar,
and might never have taken to fiction, but for the
remark of Miss Seymour, a lady acting at the Hay-

market Theatre, who, when he read to her some portion of a play he was writing, cried out, "Why don't you write novels?" It seems that Reade, like Dickens and Wilkie Collins, had a bias for the stage; and this frankness did not at the time please him, but nevertheless he *did* try his hand at fiction, and the result was *Peg Woffington* and *Christie Johnstone*. In the latter story the hero, Lord Ipsden, converses with the lower orders in compliance with a doctor's moral prescription; and here occurs the episode of the spearman, who, having only his body to shield his king in battle, gave it, as was his duty, and met the death levelled at his sovereign. The battle won, the king came to look at the dying spearman, and finding him past surgery, as the narrator says,—with two words from the royal mouth he and we were barons of Ipsden from that day to this. The whole episode is in Reade's best style, and few could read it and not feel stirred within. But it is only one of many similar fine things wherein this great novelist reminds us of Scott in his most heroic moods.

Reverting to England we need only read *Darnley*, by G. P. R. James, to gather thence a very just idea of Henry VIII. and Cardinal Wolsey.

Ten more novels have thus covered the whole of the mediæval period; and the reader who assimilates their contents should have gained thence

a good general notion of early European history
and life during that period.

But we must remember the East; and in Lord
Beaconsfield's splendid novel *Alroy* we have much
information, in the guise of fiction, as to the
Caliphate in its decline, and the desperate attempt
of what may be called the dying chivalry of the
Hebrews to restore and consolidate the ancient
kingdom of Judah.

As to the crusades themselves, there is Scott's
fine novel, the *Talisman*, introducing King Richard
the Lion-heart, and Saladin himself.

Scott's *Kenilworth* sufficiently posts us as to the
days of Queen Elizabeth; and in Charles Kingsley's *Westward Ho!* we obtain a most instructive
insight into the early days of the Spanish settle-
ments in the West Indies.

Reverting to Italy, George Eliot's *Romola* will
make much plain in Italian middle-age politics
and life; while G. P. R. James' *Arrah Neil* and
Scott's *Peveril of the Peak* give us Charles I. and
Charles II. respectively. And here I would observe
that, in making up this history of the world
through a sequence of novels, it is inevitable that
books should come into juxtaposition that are in
no wise on a level as to literary merit; but in thus
contrasting the style and general workmanship of
novelists, so very far removed the one from the

other, the reader would acquire a practical lesson in comparative literary criticism, while, at the same time, receiving useful instruction in point of taste.

Thackeray's *Esmond* should be read as well as Lord Lytton's *Devereux*, which gives us a good picture of the England of Queen Anne ; and so, too, does Miss Braddon's carefully-written *Mohawks ;* Fielding, in *Tom Jones*, affords a just idea of town and country life among the middle classes in the Georgian days ; and we may also read with advantage Besant and Rice's *Chaplain of the Fleet*, whence more information as to eighteenth-century manners and customs can be obtained ; James Grant's *Scottish Cavalier* and *Philip Rollo*—going back a little in point of time—will inform us as to things continental during the two centuries or so preceding the great French Revolution ; while in Robert Buchanan's *Shadow of the Sword* we have a grim, Dantesque kind of picture of the curse of the conscription under the Napoleonic regime. Modern India under the British rule will be found admirably portrayed in Meadows Taylor's *Confessions of a Thug*. In like manner, China—her temples, and some of the inner life of the priests—is set forth in James Payn's *By Proxy*.

So far we have some thirty-two novels, and the fact and historic information that they contain is encyclopædic in its range, and, if carefully analysed, would speedily convince the most sceptical on the point that a well-arranged course of novel reading, on a plan corresponding to that thus roughly sketched, could not fail to be fraught with very great benefit to any reader.

Let us, however, make a few additions to these thirty-two novels, which, in the guise of fiction, go so very far to give us the history of the world from the remotest times down to the present day. In the first Lord Lytton's *My Novel* we can obtain, in a most delightful way, a thorough insight into contemporary English life among the well-to-do classes, and we have, too, a great insight into Parliamentary life, and much information as to current statesmanship from a party point of view. More politics can be learned from George Eliot's *Felix Holt, the Radical;* while such a novel as David Christie Murray's *Joseph's Coat* furnishes a good insight into the domestic life and ways of our north-country ironworkers; and this may be supplemented to advantage by Besant's *All Sorts and Conditions of Men,* giving vivid delineations of life in the East End of London.

Then, if we wish to learn something of the West of England, have we not *Lorna Doone ?* And in quite a recent fiction, *Micah Clarke,* by Conan Doyle, there may be found one of the best accounts that ıas yet been given of Monmouth's Rebellion, and ɔf the battle of Sedgemoor. Some mention should ɔe made of *Maelcho*, a sixteenth-century romance 'narrated" by the Hon. Emily Lawless, the ıuthor of a fine work entitled *Grania*, and *With Essex in Ireland;* besides these there is *In Furtherst 'nd*, by Sydney Colyrier, being a romantic story of wenty years in India in the reign of Charles II.; ınd *The Crimson Sign*, by S. R. Keightley.

It may not be generally known that in the preace to the 1829 edition of the Waverley novels Sir Walter Scott refers to the fact that in 1807 he ındertook, at the request of John Murray The 3econd, to arrange for publication the posthumous works of Joseph Strutt (1749-1802), the famous ıntiquary and artist. These works included a ıistorical romance — time, Henry VI. — entitled *Queen Hoo Hall.* Sir Walter Scott, finding it ınfinished, completed the romance, of which he ɛxpressed a very high opinion; and writing thereof ıe says: "It was a step in my advance towards ːomantic composition". The possible sympathetic ɛequence of *Queen Hoo Hall* and, say, *Ivanhoe* is ɛqually curious and interesting.

Finally, reverting once more to things conti- ıental, we have in the *Parisians* of Lord Lytton a leeply-interesting and very instructive account of ːhe Third Empire prior to the Franco-German War.

CHAPTER III

THE HISTORICAL NOVEL FURTHER CONSIDERED.

THE re-issue, in popular form, of the Waverley novels, and of the historical romances of Charles Kingsley, and the sale in a short time of over a million of copies thereof, are surely events, if not epochs, in the development of latter nineteenth-century literary taste. For one thing it is very clearly shown that there is a public—probably one of the young—for historical romance, a branch of fiction which some time back threatened, so the publishers declared, to be like poetry—a drug in the market. The Waverley novels—some thirty in number—are more than two-thirds historical, and comprise stirring periods in Scottish, English, and continental literature, from the Conquest to the close of the Jacobite struggle with the House of Hanover. No doubt the historical novel had gone much out of fashion, but this was simply from lack of supply, not through failure of demand; and the advent of a generation of young readers has been

1arked by a decided revival of the old taste that
1ade the successive issues of Scott's and subse-
uently of the first Lord Lytton's, historic novels
vents in the reading world during the first half of
he nineteenth century.

History, when popularised, compensates in some
ense for the shortness of life, and for the limits
/hich preclude most of us from reading the past
hrough the more fascinating medium of travel;
nd certainly, when crystallised in artistic fiction
y the really skilful novelist, affords an enjoyment
ɔ most readers at ọnce rare, continual, and in-
ensely dramatic.

Of historical novelists Sir Walter Scott is un-
uestionably the greatest, just as Shakespeare is
he greatest of dramatic poets. Some attempts
ave been made to detract from the author of
vanhoe; and we all know how it has been said
hat Scott has no subjectivity, that he deals only
/ith the outside of life, and has left to others the
ubtle analysis of motive, and, indeed, all that is
ntrospective and metaphysical. This, like most
weeping criticism, is not wholly true. To draw,
s Scott does, the objective forms of human life is
ecidedly to *suggest* the subjective side too; and,
ι truth, to delineate as perfectly as he does, real
ιen and women, both in repose and in action, is to
ome nearer to the ideal of great fiction than to

give merely groups of what a writer imagines to be
the secret springs and source of human conduct.
The former are necessarily far nearer the truth
than the latter, which often lack reality, and are
clothed with the dress, rather than the nature, of
humanity.

It has been alleged, too, that Scott is often in-
accurate; but history itself is full of uncertainties,
and what Carlyle would rightly call its verities are
not at all dependent on a date or a name, or even
a particular place. It is exactly thus with Shakespeare, who has so often moulded history to the
exigencies of an art more consummate than can
be found in the most exactly classic production,
having not one anachronism, and a perfect con-
formity to all the dramatic unities.

No one, before or since, has had so wide and
varied a range, and so firm a grasp of realism,
always tempered with poetic ideality, as Scott;
yet it must be confessed that if in *Ivanhoe* and the
Fair Maid of Perth Scott has produced the best of
all our true historical novels, he probably wrote
the worst, however, in *Count Robert of Paris* and
Anne of Geierstein.

There is in Scott not only the healthy mind,
but that true elevation of character which constitutes, after all, the most enduring charm of the
great mass of fiction that he has left behind him.

owhere in his pages can aught be found that in
ay way tends to lower the tone of any reader;
n the contrary, in even his inferior works he is
'er lifting us to higher and nobler planes. His in-
rior, I say; for Scott produced some weak novels,
ad the distance between his lowest and highest
vel is very great indeed. Withal, however,
hatever was his theme, he ever sustained himself
y the conscious pride of race, of race in its noblest
hase, whereby is meant the selection which
aakes the true and enduring aristocracy which
rises from real personal merit, and commands
niversal homage. Scott, indeed, carried his
abit, for habit it is, of chivalric posing into nearly
ll that he produced; and he never loses sight of
ae fact that men are not equal by birth. Some
re born to higher planes as inevitably as some to
)wer planes of action; and until men recognise
his, true social reform must ever be one of the
aost difficult forms of progress to achieve. The
act is, all Scott's sympathy went out to the grand
ide of life, and for him it was impossible to feel
rue interest in aught that is sordid and ignoble.
Iis whole tone is pitched to the keynote sounded
a a stanza of a ballad he wrote entitled *Helvellyn*,
/hich commemorates the incident of a traveller,
vho, losing his way, perished on the mountain in
805. The stanza runs :—

When a prince to the fate of the peasant has yielded,
  The tapestry waves round the dim lighted hall ;
With scutcheons of silver the coffin is shielded,
  And pages stand mute by the canopied pall.
Through the courts at deep midnight the torches are
  gleaming,
In the proudly arched chapel the banners are beaming,
Far down the long aisle sacred music is streaming,
  Lamenting a chief of the people should fall !

I think those lines convey to us a very correct idea of the ruling passion in Scott and of the spirit that pervaded his whole life. He belongs in a sense to the chivalric past, and embodies in himself all that was best, purest, and noblest of the feudalism he loved to delineate.

In *Ivanhoe*, introducing Richard Cœur de Lion, the weak and wicked John, and showing the final flicker of the fiery struggle between Saxon and Norman, we have views of England during the early feudal times, equally instructive and entertaining. Chivalry appears in full panoply and great splendour, and the pictures given of the Knights Templar alone stamp the romance as a masterpiece. Then, beyond all the pageantry and the stress of a terrible strife, in Wamba, Scott ascends fully to the Shakespearian plane ; and while he draws true fun from the Saxon fool, he subtly shows the human heart beneath the garb of the professional jester, and gives us a man where lesser

·iters can accomplish only a mask. In the Hebrew
aiden, too, we cannot fail to recognise a con-
ption tender as that of Cordelia herself, but
:engthened with the heroism of the race that
oduced Jephtha's daughter and Miriam ; and the
ost gorgeous of English romances closes, for all
no can sympathise with female purity and devo-
on, with a mist of tears, through which is seen
e rainbow promise of the great Hereafter.

Quite on a level with *Ivanhoe*, but how different
every detail, is the *Fair Maid of Perth*. This is
novel, perhaps, even now not so well understood
it should be ; for it belongs undoubtedly to the
st period of Scott's constructive genius, when all
s powers for delineating human passions were at
eir maximum. It is a terrible reproduction of a
arful phase of Scottish history ; and in Ian Eachin
ac Ian (the Conachar of the story) we have—what
rare in Scott—a combination of the subjective
ement with the objective. Conachar is a youth
lly conscious of all his ancestral glory, but con-
itutionally and physically a coward. He is aware
his infirmity—an appalling affliction in such an
;e—and the mental torture resulting thence, and
lminating in his tragic fate, is throughout on the
ane of ancient Greek tragedy. Nay, it is even
·eater in this—that in no part of the narrative
Conachar does he soar, as some of the Greek

heroes, beyond the warm touch of our common human nature; and even when we most despise, we most pity the unhappy chief, who, at the head of his clan, sees his foster brothers fall around him one by one, dying in his defence, and yet *cannot* risk his life to save or avenge them! Both in conception and execution, Scott has here surpassed himself; and yet Conachar is but one of many portraitures as lifelike as his. The Homeric battle too, of the clans Quhele and Chattan, is only one of many magnificent episodes in a romance which includes some of the most splendid panoramic scenes in literature of this type. Henry Gow, the famous smith; the boastful poltroon, Master Oliver Proudfute; the snake-like Pottingar, who heals or poisons with equal indifference; Sir John Ramorny, the man of the world of the day, unscrupulous, bold, and base, and yet in some respects a man of knightly mark; the brutal Bonthron; then again the Duke of Rothsay, weak and vicious, yet a prince—these are but some of the *dramatis personæ* of this romance, so opulent in distinctive human portraiture. Besides all these, we have King Robert; the terrible Douglas of that day, feeling and asserting himself as more than a king; the plotting Duke of Albany; Prior Anselm, a finished delineation of the typical ecclesiastic of that period; the honest glover imself, and many others. Then, in female ortraiture, there is the fair maid herself, and ouise, the wandering glee maiden, who through- ut rouses and retains the sympathy of every ader. The intervals between the great episodes f the story are filled by numberless incidents, and owhere is there a trace of that artificiality which apparent even in such fine work as the *Harold* f the first Lord Lytton. No, the whole narrative ours tumultuously forth, and each event in its apid course has for its great justification the fact at it is there. We no more question the arrange- ent than we do that of the sinuosities of a wind- g river, although we immediately detect faults hat may exist in the cutting out of the artificial tream that is made to meander through some ewly-made pleasure grounds.

In *Quentin Durward*, an inferior work by far to ither *Ivanhoe* or the *Fair Maid of Perth*, there is, owever, a highly-finished portraiture of the crafty ouis XI.

Of the Waverley historical novels, seven are ssentially English. In the *Betrothed*—weak in elation to Scott's best work, but in itself a ro- nance of much interest—we have a vivid present- nent of the wars with the Welsh. The *Talisman* s thoroughly English, although the scene is laid n Syria, and besides the lifelike delineation of

3

Richard I., there is Saladin himself limned with a master hand. *Ivanhoe* has already been dealt with, and thence we leap on to *Kenilworth*, with its fine Elizabethan characters, and the great Queen herself as the centre of all. In the *Fortunes of Nigel* a rather minute description is given of the period of James I.; and among the strong points of the book is the realistic sketch of " Alsatia," the London waterside stronghold of the town ruffianism of that time. In *Woodstock* appear Cromwell and Charles II., both faithful portraitures; and then, what can be more affecting and true to nature than Sir Henry Lee and his pathetic end, as the joyous pageantry of the Restoration, for which he had suffered so long and so heroically, flashes in upon his dying eyes? In *Peveril of the Peak* the reign of the dissolute Charles is delineated with the greatest fidelity to fact, and the society of the period is brought before the reader in vivid colours, and with consummate scenic skill.

Of the purely Scottish novels there are just eight. The earliest in date of story (not in production) is about the worst book Scott wrote. This is *Castle Dangerous*, dealing with the great Douglas family in the days of Edward I. Of the *Fair Maid of Perth* I have fully spoken above; and next in order of date come two fine novels, the *Monastery* and the *Abbot*, both having for their central figure

:he unhappy Queen of Scots. Then comes the
splendid *Legend of Montrose*, including the best
type of a true soldier of fortune—Dugald Dalgety
—in all fiction. We now pass to *Old Mortality*,
with its stern and faithful delineations of the grim
Covenanters ; while in *Waverley* the Pretender appears very much as he was, and in *Red Gauntlet*
the last spark of the Jacobite rebellion goes out
into utter darkness.

Properly speaking, only three of the Waverley
novels deal with continental history; these are
Count Robert of Paris, relating to the declining
days of the Eastern Empire; *Quentin Durward*,
depicting the struggle of Louis XI. with Charles
the Bold of Burgundy; and, finally, *Anne of
Geierstein*, wherein we have much of Swiss patriotism of the same period.

It is not too much to affirm that, except in
Shakespeare, nowhere in imaginative literature
can such a varied gallery of historic portraits be
found—portraits instinct with life, and drawn with
a fidelity to nature which royally atones for a few
deviations from the dry-as-dust statistics and
facts which constitute only the skeleton of history,
and tell us as much about it as an anatomical
museum does of human character. Contemporary
with, and immediately successive to, Scott, were
some other historic novelists, who are naturally

dwarfed by his Homeric stature and Shakespearian wealth of incident, description, and dialogue.

Then, far indeed below even the lower plane of
Scott's genius, come the historical novels of the
sisters Anna Maria and Jane Porter. The former
was a sort of pupil of the great Sir Walter, whom
she knew in her youth, and in her *Hungarian
Brothers*, *Recluse of Norway*, and the *Knights of
St. John*, there is really much to admire, as well
as to interest. Jane Porter took up the legendary
stories of William Wallace, which Scott rather
curiously overlooked; and under the title of the
Scottish Chiefs, a novel of power, traces out with
much historic accuracy the whole career of the
unhappy patriot, to whom fiction, perhaps, has done
but scant justice.

Occupying a far lower plane, although exceedingly popular in their day, were the many novels
of George Payne Rainsford James, who, in a series
of well-constructed stories, covered a great extent
of historic ground. Thus, in *Forest Days* we have
the reign of Henry III. and the opening of that of
Edward I.; in *Agincourt* Henry V. appears, and in
Arrah Neil, a pathetic novel, Charles I. is one of
the actors. In *Philip Augustus* James deals with
the most splendid periods of French and Flemish
history, and this novel includes a really spirited

description of the great battle of Bovines. In *Attila* will be found a series of vivid pictures from the decline and fall of the Roman Empire, while the terrible Hun is presented to the reader with much realistic skill. In *Richelieu, Henry of Guise,* and the *Ancien Régime,* bright and interesting views are given of France under the old *noblesse;* and in the *Jacquerie* an attempt is made to paint one of the greatest social convulsions of the middle ages.

It has been much the fashion to deride James, but it cannot be denied that he is one of the purest of novelists, and he often succeeds in calling back the vanished past, with much of its pomp and pageantry; and, while entirely devoid of the coarseness which disfigures some of the novels of the author of *Jack Sheppard,* he is to the full as sensational.

Harrison Ainsworth, indeed, is on a lower plane, like James Grant, although both writers have had great popularity, which was, perhaps, mainly due to the fact that history, in its picturesque and stirring phases, *does* interest readers at all times, whatever some literary specialists may allege to the contrary.

Far beyond all these writers, and lower only than Scott himself, is the first Lord Lytton, who produced in *Harold, the Last of the Saxon Kings,* what is almost worthy to be called a prose epic.

The description given of the battles of Stamford
Bridge and of Hastings is very fine, and, however
doubtful may be the historic facts, the closing
pages of *Harold* can be read by few unmoved,
while, ever and anon, the prose becomes really impassioned blank verse, and is instinct with noble
sentiments and true pathos. In the *Last of the
Barons* we have a stirring account of the closing
struggle in England between the feudal lords and
the trading classes, supported by the Crown.

Lord Lytton also wrote *Rienzi*, wherein Italy
during the middle ages is powerfully sketched;
and in *Leila, or the Siege of Granada,* we have a
fine monograph on the downfall of the Moslem
dominion in Spain.

A very notable historical novelist was the late
Major Whyte Melville, who, although a writer of
sporting and "society" fiction, produced, at all
events, one masterpiece in the *Gladiators*, a tale of
ancient Rome. In this work a wide and often
gorgeous canvas is unrolled before the reader. It
includes vivid but faithful pictures of the imperial
city already declining, but still irradiated with fitful
flashes of valour, and even of virtue. The awful
siege of Jerusalem and the destruction of the Temple
are among the great episodes; and these, with other
historic events, are worked with great skill into the
very woof of the narrative. Some of the characters,

too, are highly-finished studies; as in Julius Placidus, the Roman statesman, conspirator and gentleman, he reminds one of Horace and Juvenal in prose; while the haughty and handsome Valeria and the tender Marianne are delightful transcripts of real women. The "family" of gladiators is limned with the force of a Rubens, and all that fidelity to detail which is found in the best Flemish painters of still life. The *Gladiators* is a great book, and it is a historical novel too, which excites in the reader sympathy, a thing that inferior work of this kind rarely rouses. Then, in some respects on a plane with this, are the historic novels of Charles Kingsley. In *Hereward the Wake* we have a sort of sequel to the late Lord Lytton's *Harold;* but it is in *Westward Ho!* that Kingsley is at his brightest and best. The canvas is spread wide, and the faithful portraitures of men like Sir Richard Grenville, the knightly Amyas (a conception worthy of Spenser himself), of Yeo (that man of might), of Don Guzman the proud, and many more, render his book a wondrous panorama of the most stirring times that England has ever known. Then, what a Viking-like feast there is of gallant but generous fighting, and how vivid is the colouring of the scenes in South America! In some respects *Westward Ho!* is a national prose epic. The sea-fights are worthy of Marryat; and then there are the

Rembrandt-like pictures of the fell Inquisition in the New World.

Another remarkable historic novel of Kingsley's is *Hypatia*, wherein is vivified with a touch of real genius the manners, the customs, and the people of the fifth century.   Hypatia, the heroine, the daughter of Theon, an Alexandrine astronomer, and head of the Neoplatonic school of that famous . city, was really a miracle of beauty and learning, and, in some respects, anticipated the modern woman's intellectual movement by fifteen centuries. Hypatia propounded metaphysics, that pagan in mould were Christian in substance ; but by Cyril, the Bishop of Alexandria, she was regarded as a Satanically-inspired pythoness.   In the issue this led to the tragedy set forth in Kingsley's pages with so much power and realism.   Much may be learned, indeed, from Kingsley's *Hypatia* relative to the influence of the Orient on the Greek mind, and to the way in which the corruption of early Christianity in the East prepared the way for the strong, simple, and sincere theism of Mahomet. History, philosophy, poetry, and romance are here blended with a consummate art into a glowing gorgeous tissue.   The ordinary life of Alexandria is etched in with a Frith-like fidelity to fact, and it is coloured with a richness reminding us of Paul Veronese.   The sports of the favourite Alexandrian

:rena are finely delineated, and the rising of Aphro-
lite is a piece of word-painting not easily matched
n our romantic fiction.   Then amid all we have
he glorious figure of Hypatia, in her bloom of
)eauty and regal power of intellect, as the centre
)f a piece of really splendid historic romance.

Returning to English ground, we must not pass
)ver *Lorna Doone*, Mr. R. D. Blackmore's remark-
ıble romance, which by 1882 had reached (it was
ssued in 1869) a twentieth edition.   This novel
ransports us to the days of James II., the hapless
Vlonmouth, the infamous Jeffreys, and the yet
nore infamous Colonel Kirke ; and in recounting
he savage deeds of the outlawed Doones in the
iepths of Bagworthy forest, the beauty and charm-
ng character of the heroine, Lorna, the Herculean
:trength and robust honesty of John Ridd, to say
ıothing of Tom Faggus, we have a treat indeed.
_ord Russell, and the pure, proud, ancient Roman-
ike Algernon Sydney, figure in the story, which is
' set " in a world of natural loveliness, and teems
vith incident and episode.   Then, how clear and
:trong is the word-picture drawn of the fatal field
)f Sedgemoor, when, as the narrative says, "noble
:ountrymen, armed with scythe, pickaxe, black-
;mith's hammer, or fold pitchers, stood for hours
ıgainst blazing musketry and deadly cannon ;
ıgainst men they could not get at by reason of

the water-dykes, shouting out, 'Cross the rhaine, and coom within reache!'" The personal combat between Carver Doone and the hero is certainly one of the most tremendous things in fiction, and parallels every way the fearful fight between Bothwell and Balfour in Scott's *Old Mortality*.

Curiously enough, the rebellion of the West has lately proved attractive to other novelists seeking historic groundwork for their plots. Mr. Walter Besant has produced, in his *For Faith and Freedom*, a fine variation on the historic lines taken up by Blackmore; and Mr. Conan Doyle, in *Micah Clarke*, gives us an even more detailed account of the Monmouth rising, introducing therein a soldier of fortune—Decimus Saxon—worthy to take a place beside Dugald Dalgety in Scott's *Legend of Montrose*, while later Mr. Hume Nisbet has done so in his novel *Her Loving Slave*.

In *For Faith and Freedom* the opening deals with the historic expulsion of some 2000 ministers from their livings for conscience sake, that black Bartholomew of England, as it has been called, in contradistinction to the red one of France. Alice Eykin, the heroine, rouses the sympathy of the reader, and the exile portion of the novel is excellent.

In *Micah Clarke* all the writer's force has been concentrated on the battle piece, much of which is in words that move us like the long roll of the drum. The onset of the Life Guards is thus described: " Close to us the Taunton men had hardened into a dark sullen ring, bristling with steel, in the centre of which might be seen and heard their venerable leader, his long beard fluttering in the breeze. . . . Louder and louder grew the roar of the horse. ' Steady, my lads ! ' cried Saxon, in trumpet tones. ' Give not an inch ! ' A great shout went up, and then the living wave broke over us." The rest is Homeric. Finally, "the cloud of horsemen recoiled, circling all over the plain, and the shout of triumph proclaimed that we had seen the backs of as stout a squadron as ever followed kettle-drums ".

Since writing *Micah Clarke*, the author, Mr. Conan Doyle, has produced another historical novel relative to the wars of Edward III., entitled the *White Company*; and later he has produced the *Refugees*. This story is laid at the period of the Revocation of the Edict of Nantes. The principal characters are Huguenots; but Louis XIV. is introduced, and Madame Maintenon; while Bossuet, Fénelon, Corneille, Condé, and the Minister Louvois are all well etched in. The third volume gives the adventures of the refugees in the wilds of North America; and among the creations of the book is decidedly the young New Englander Amos Green. There is a great wealth of detailed description cleverly worked into the very tissue of this fine romance. The account given of a levee of the great king is undoubtedly equally interesting and instructive; and in working out his conception of Louis XIV., Mr. Doyle has laid a great mass of facts under heavy contribution.

Mention may be made here of Mr. Stanley Weyman, who has quite lately come to the front as a writer of good historical romance. His three-volumed romance, entitled *A Gentleman of France*, is a sort of chronicle of an imaginary personage, but one presented with much vivid verisimilitude, and known as Gaston de Bonne, Sieur de Marsac. This gentleman of France is no youthful hero, but a mature man of forty, and he is cunningly worked into a web of intrigue. Among the characters introduced are Henry of Navarre and Vicomte de Turenne; while assassinations, fighting with the sword, and a great variety of thrilling incidents, have been incorporated with a very interesting romance. A later novel by the same writer is entitled *Under the Red Robe*.

Among brilliant revivalists of the romantic and historic past, mention is due to Edna Lyall's beautiful conception, *In the Golden Days*, wherein Algernon Sydney, that noble victim of the Rye House Plot, is presented to the reader in his habit as he lived. Sydney was a man of Catonian mould; and in Edna

ᴧyall's graphic pages he lives again, and may be
tudied anew amid his favourite surroundings at
Knowle Park. A later work yet of Edna Lyall's
� a three-volumed novel, called *To Right the
Vrong*, wherein the hero is made a parliamen-
arian in the days of the great Rebellion, thus
eversing the usual order in fiction, which pre-
ented the Cavaliers as more or less white and the
Roundheads as more or less black.

"Edna Lyall," it is well to mention, is a daughter
f the late Robert Bayly, of the Inner Temple,
ᵢarrister-at-law. She was born and educated at
Brighton, and took to writing fiction at an early age.
Her first story, *Won by Waiting*, appeared in 1879.

Quite out of the common track of ordinary his-
oric novels is such a work as *John Inglesant*, by
. H. Shorthouse. This novel practically narrates
ᵥhat is put forth as the true story of a young
ᵢnglishman named Inglesant, a servant of Charles
. Inglesant is described as closely connected with
he Roman Catholics of these troubled times, and
e is employed in sundry secret negotiations be-
ween the ill-starred King and the Catholic gentry.
'he story pivots on the singular murder of John's
nly brother, who resembles him in a twin-like
ᵣanner. In opening up all this, however, there
ᵢ much to interest those who love to see mentally
he processional pageantry of the gorgeous past,

and the reader is here carried back to Henry VIII.
The education of John is well described. It is
such as was prescribed for youths who were to be
practically taught the doctrine of implicit obedi-
ence; and we are here introduced to Hobbes, the
philosopher of Malmesbury, in his habit as he
lived. Some part of the novel leans to the occult,
as in the powerful episode describing the dreadful
appearance of Lord Strafford to the remorseful
King, two days after the execution of the former.
The tragedy of the King himself is finely described; and then, when the scene shifts to Italy,
a new set of historic incidents comes into play.
There are some awful scenes in John Inglesant's
married life, and throughout the work fiction and
history are blended with considerable art.

Among recent historical classical novels may be
mentioned, too, Mr. Alfred Clarke's stirring narrative, *Woe to the Conquered* (B.C. 71-1). Here we
have in dramatic form slaves, gladiators and
Roman ladies very much after the fashion of the
first Lord Lytton in the *Last Days of Pompeii.*

Mr. E. C. Adams has lately attracted some
notice by a book called *The Bow and the Sword,*
wherein the ancient Persians are brought before
the reader in a fiction which, like some of Mr.
Rider Haggard's work, is based on many carefully
compiled historic facts.

The utilities fully equal the pleasures of historical novel reading, great as the latter are. More especially does the historical novel become important as an agency of culture in days when separatism, and individualism, and class distinctions all tend to become more accentuated. But for the agency of the newspaper, indeed, the circumscribed character of the lives of many even of those who have means would be intolerable. In the middle ages classes were much more in contact than now, and even the low-born sometimes penetrated into noble, and even Court circles. Kings occasionally mingled with the people, and the nobility did so to a considerable extent. The fact is, rank was then so distinctly and permanently defined, that the high-born had no fear of losing caste by a little familiarity with their natural inferiors ; and, consequently, sympathies were fostered between the high and low, which do not exist now. As a rule, persons of any pretence to intellect lived in feudal days lives richer in personal variety than most of the middle classes do now; for in these days persons generally mix most exclusively with those of their own station, and thus the social divisions of contemporary life are true strata, that separate only, and but rarely interpenetrate.

Every feudal castle was a little court, a small kingdom, with its sovereign, nobles, church, and army, and thus the pomp and pageantry of high life, were brought home to all classes much more than is the case now.   Thus it may be truly said that in the reading of good historical novels, lies the true corrective to the essentially prosaic and selfish side of contemporary life; and in the chivalry and heroism of the glorious past, as set forth in the golden and highly-coloured pages of good, romantic historic fiction, we find a real antidote for much of the pessimistic materialism of our own day.

Few persons, comparatively speaking, know the fulness wherewith even English history has been dealt with in various forms of historic fiction. We might, indeed, easily construct a continuous chronicle of British history if we took, in chrono-logical order, those writers who among them have seized on, and more or less vivified, all periods of our " rough island story ".

Naturally, if such a course of historic novels be prescribed, we must be content to take a sequence of writers of altogether unequal power, ranging from some scarcely, if at all, above mediocrity, to the supreme genius of Scott himself.   But, to give some idea of the way in which British history might be studied uninterruptedly in fiction, we will cite a few examples.   The second century in those islands of the Christian era has been treated by " A.L.O.E.'

in *Daybreak in Britain*, illustrative of early Christianity; and the late Mr. W. H. G. Kingston, in *Edol, the Druid*, deals with the same subject. Dr. Cutts describes the Roman occupation, in the *Villa of Claudius*, while the missions of St. Augustine are treated in the *Early Dawn* and in *Imogen*, by Mrs. Charles and Emily S. Holt respectively. Then Dr. Cutts again, in *St. Cedd's Cross*, touches on Saxon Christianity in the seventh century; and the late Edwin Atherstone paints the state of things here in the ninth century in his *Sea Kings of England*. The late Charles Mackay grapples with the Norman Conquest, supplementing Lord Lytton's *Harold*, in the *Camp of Refuge;* and the same period is dealt with in an infinitely finer manner by Charles Kingsley in *Hereward the Wake*, of whom it was traditionally said that three such men would have undone the Conquest and expelled the Normans! Mrs. Maberley, in the *Lady and the Priest*, tells the story of Henry, Rosamond, and Thomas à Becket.

The twelfth century is delineated by Julia Corner in the *King and the Troubadour; Ivanhoe* has already been cited here; and the barons' wars are duly set forth in the *Siege of Kenilworth*, by L. S. Stanhope; while Miss C. M. Yonge, in the *Lances of Lynwood*, brings the Black Prince before the reader. Agnes Giberne, in *Coulyng Castle*, narrates

4

the tragic story of Sir John Oldcastle; and so we can continue the sequence down to such works as those of the late Major Whyte Melville, dealing with the ill-fated White King, or, coming to our own time, with the Crimean War, as in the *Interpreter*.

It is not needful to particularise further. It is enough to suggest how history may be intelligently and delightfully studied through the medium of the historic novel. There, too, it is certain that the higher and more enduring verities of history—the ethics thereof, indeed—may frequently be found, far more than in the pages of the professional historian. There may be in the latter more accuracy (though much sober history is of questionable authenticity, if criticised as men now criticise the Bible); but there will be less of humanity, and the lessons acquired from good historic fiction are far more salutary. It is here that we may, indeed, find a charming contrast to our more convenient, but infinitely more prosaic, present-day life, and a corrective, too, to the meanness and the narrow-mindedness too often engendered by the minute detail, and the nice subdivision of labour, which do more than aught else to belittle nineteenth-century civilisation. It is, indeed, only in the charmed and charming pages of the history as presented by the competent novelist that we can

> Fully draw that true heroic breath
> Of Spenser, Shakespeare, and Elizabeth!

CHAPTER IV

MILITARY NOVELS.

MILITARY novels have always been popular. The exercise a natural fascination on all classes c readers, and this is partly due to the fact that th life and ordinary work and recreation of the soldie are quite outside the range of ordinary knowledg How many of us are familiar with the domesti arrangements of a barrack, or the routine of drill We rarely see soldiers, as it were, at home, an they are, in a word, to the vast majority of readers a people quite apart, separate, and distinct— another race, as it were; and this, I take it, is on of the various reasons why the novel military ha ever been a general favourite.

Then, beyond all this, it is unquestionable tha most persons like, more or less, to read of war whatever may be its particular phase. Everybod knows that those portions of history which excit most interest are those relative to battle and sieg and strategy. Thus it has ever been that, in spit of philosophy, wisdom, and religion, all combining to proclaim the wickedness and folly of war, the military novel has always been, as it is now with many, a favourite form of fiction.

We have been told, indeed, that a soldier is

> A mere tool, a kind
> Of human sword in a fiend's hand ;

while war itself has been stigmatised as the sink of all injustice, the very greatest plague of the world, any scourge being preferable thereto. Byron has dashed off in four lines a frightful picture of the war-fiend—

> See where the giant on the mountain stands,
>   His blood-red tresses deepening in the sun,
> With death-shot glowing in his fiery hands,
>   And eye that scorches all it glares upon !

It has been said, too, that—

> Battle is murder on a larger scale,
> And only makes a more stupendous sin !

And it has been sarcastically asked—

> When doth Religion to such zeal attain,
> As in *Te Deums* over thousands slain ?

And yet, in spite of all this, and much more, the novel military maintains, and is likely to keep, a very favourite and foremost place in the ranks of fiction ; and truly we must not lose sight of the noble, heroic, and the self-sacrificing side of war, or its power for drawing forth some of the finest virtues of mankind. Heroism has been justly

called the divine relation, which in all time unites
a great man with other men; and has it not been
said that a noble cause ennobles warfare? At all
events it is certain that the pomp and circumstance
of glorious war—the spirit-stirring drum and the
shrill fife—still move the hearts of the multitude
like wine; and then the great Sir Walter exclaims,
in one of his martial moods—

> Swell the clarion, sound the fife !
> Unto a sensual world proclaim—
> One crowded hour of glorious life
> Is worth a world without a name !

I have my own views about war, which I will
not obtrude here; but, these aside, it is evident
that our military novelists are among our most
popular writers; and I confess that from their pages,
often instinct with wonderful dramatic power, much
may be learned of history that is well worth ac-
quiring, and which, by the way, is rarely acquired
by the average reader, except through the fascinating medium of the military novel.

Defoe—that father of our British novelists—
wrote several military novels, of which *Colonel
Jack* is a type; but it was the Napoleonic wars
that gave the great impulse to military fiction. In
a word, the majority of our military novelists are
distinctly nineteenth-century men. One of the
most prolific is Charles Lever, whose *Charles*

O'Malley, Jack Hinton, Tom Burke, Harry Lorrequer, and others, form a kind of parallel literature to the fine nautical novels of Captain Marryat.

Lever too, like Marryat, had a fine flow of animal spirits, and many of his stories rush on in a wild whirl of totally original incidents, which renders the plot of very minor moment. It must be admitted that Lever does not depend alone for the interests of his novels on the battle and siege pieces worked up, and in many of his best military novels the fighting element is but small. It is remarkable enough that in almost everything he wrote—and his works form quite a small library —he almost always has at least one remarkable example of skilled horsemanship.

After Lever comes James Grant, whose father actually served in the Peninsular War, and whose education was conducted in barracks. Thus it came about that the future novelist literally grew up in the midst of everything military. In 1839 he became an ensign in the 62nd Foot, and he actually served for some years, ultimately leaving the army in order to devote himself to literature. His first work, the *Romance of War*, dealt with the experiences of the principal Scotch regiments in the Peninsular War, and at once proved that the writer knew his subject thoroughly. Then came the *Aide-de-Camp*, the *Scottish Cavalier*, *Philip Rollo,* the *Phantom Regiment* (a weird legend of "the Butcher Cumberland, who won the Battle of Culloden"), and *Culloden*, and very many more.

Apart from the great interest that centres in all these novels, not a little may be learned thence relative to the military history of Europe during the past two or three centuries; for in *Philip Rollo* we have Count Tilley and the veterans of the famous Thirty Years' War. In his later novels the writer deals with such comparatively recent episodes as the Indian Mutiny, and in the latest works of all we have our "little wars" duly set forth almost up to date.

Another military novelist well worthy of the title is Gleig. Originally he too served in the Peninsular War, and subsequently in the short, sharp American War of 1812. Retiring on half-pay, he eventually entered the Church, and, when in orders, began to write, producing some very effective novels, embodying, more or less, his own experiences. One of these novels, the *Subaltern*, gives a very correct idea of the young officer's life in days when purchase reigned supreme, and the present system of competitive examinations was unknown.

Very much on a level with Gleig, is W. H. Maxwell, the author of *Hector O'Halloran*, and the *Bivouac*, wherein a number of military tales are clustered on a slender thread of narrative, and several other novels of very much the same type.

Then the late Major Whyte Melville, the author of the *Gladiators*, that fine romance of ancient Rome and of Judæa, wrote several good military novels.

Miss Louise Ramée ("Ouida"), who is generally to be reckoned as among poetic novelists, has produced two or three specially military novels, of which *Under Two Flags* is, perhaps, on the whole the best. Very much satire, and even ridicule, has been heaped on this writer's descriptions of English guardsmen and their extravagant follies; and yet, although Ouida is often surprisingly at fault, it is certain that many of the sketches she has made of the effeminate and utterly spendthrift "curled darlings" who may be found in crack corps, are true to the life.

"John Strange Winter" is the name under which Mrs. Arthur Stannard (1856) writes. Among her most noteworthy novels are *Bootles' Baby* (1885), a production supposed at first by the world to have been written by a cavalry officer, *On March, Army Society*, and others.

This writer most certainly possesses much exact acquaintance with barrack life, and has created a form of military novel almost special to herself.

She does not in the least depend on the pomp and circumstance of war, but interests us in the daily life and the domestic affairs of officers and men living in barracks, and that generally under conditions of peace. This writer, too, has the art of introducing little children, and rendering them naturally, and, therefore, making them really interesting.

By the way, it is curious that while in *Vanity Fair* Thackeray avoids any attempt to deal with Waterloo, and declares his place to be with the women and the baggage, he did, in *Barry Lyndon*, that strange novel of adventure, give us much relative to military affairs; and this is well done too. Perhaps this particular book is less generally known than any other of Thackeray's minor fictions.

The late Captain Hawley Smart wrote a goodly number of novels having military men among the principal characters; but most of his fiction is rather a record of sporting life, than a series of transcripts from the camp and battle-field. Among his principal works are *Play or Pay, Hard Lines, From Post to Finish, Saddle and Sabre*.

Among those who of late have taken up the military novel in relation to actual war, is Mr. George Alfred Henty. He saw some service in the purveying department in the Crimea, and after organising military hospitals, he became a war-correspondent to the *Standard* newspaper.   He witnessed the Italo-Austrian War and was with Garibaldi.   Mr. Henty also shared in the Ashantee Expedition and in the Franco-German War.   He has turned this experience to good account in such fiction as the *March to Coomassie*, the *March to Magdala*, and the *Young Franc Tireurs*—fiction, however, which is very largely composed of fact, and is all the more interesting on that account.

CHAPTER V

NAVAL AND NAUTICAL NOVELS.

FROM many causes, at all times, the sea has had an intense charm for Anglo-Saxons. This is the result of temperament, tradition, environment, and a thousand associations, each of which is a spell of magic power. Byron declares that—

> There is society where none intrudes,
> By the deep sea, and music in its roar;

and probably, as the earth generally becomes more and more explored and fully occupied, the pathless wastes of the unfathomable deep, with all the phenomena peculiar to the ocean wastes a thousand leagues from shore, will exercise a yet more fascinating influence on the imagination.

We have been told that, after all, earth has no plain so beautiful as that of the sea, rightly viewed; and the many mysteries of the ocean, engulfed cities, buried continents, to say nothing of the argosies of commerce, or the battle-ships that have gone down in a blaze of red ruin, all combine to weave a charm which impels many to take up preferentially any form of fiction dealing with the sea in any of its myriad aspects.

A writer has said that to be at sea, withdrawn out of the reach of the innumerable temptations of the world, with full opportunity to observe the wonders of God in the great deep, is a vast help to quicken the life of faith; and certainly, whatever it be now, in the days of long voyages sailors were on the whole a more reverent class of men than soldiers.

Many writers of fiction during the present century have treated the sea in an episodic sense, as Victor Hugo, in his *Toilers of the Sea;* but it is, perhaps, a little strange that the number of British novelists who have made the sea their special theme is by no means so great as might be expected. This is undoubtedly due to the fact that real success in nautical literature can be attained only by a writer who has actually lived on the sea, and been in close contact with sailors. The first writer of fiction to describe the sea effectively was certainly Defoe, as witness the really fine description given of the ocean in various parts of *Robinson Crusoe.* Defoe, however, had little or no experience of his own; and the first novelist who has given us life at sea from his own personal observation was Tobias Smollett, who served as a surgeon in the Royal Navy; and in *Roderick Random,* published in 1748, painted some pictures of life on board a king's ship which are much more graphic than pleasing. James Fenimore Cooper (more fully noticed under "American Novels") wrote several sea tales. He had served himself in the American Navy, but only for six years, when he deserted the sea, married, and took to literature. Cooper wrote *The Pilot*, which contains the first sketch of a typical American seaman, in the character of "Long Tom Coffin".

The greatest of all who have written purely sea stories is unquestionably, so far, Captain Frederick Marryat, who, before he wrote a line, served in the Royal Navy, especially in the famous *Impérieuse*, commanded then by Lord Cochrane. Under this celebrated fighting officer young Marryat is said to have been engaged, between 1806 and 1809, in over fifty engagements; and such was his valour and general good conduct that he became commander in 1815; and it was not until 1832, at the age of forty, that this daring seaman, who had five times rescued sailors from drowning, and had been frequently and most honourably mentioned in despatches, took up the novelist's pen. He soon began to pour forth in rapid succession a series of really excellent novels, nearly all devoted to life at sea. *Peter Simple*, *Jacob Faithful*, *The King's Own*, *The Pirate and*

Three Cutters, are all in their several ways master-pieces ; while in *Midshipman Easy* we have, perhaps, the only true nautical screaming farce bound up within the covers of a naval novel.   The variety of characters depicted from able seamen upward, through all grades of the service, to say nothing of accessory personages in his generally extensive *dramatis personæ*, is simply astounding, while the descriptions given of almost all forms of naval warfare and enterprise, are exactly in the manner of one who was narrating facts, as, indeed, he generally did in the guise of fiction.   Then, making due allowance for the roughness of those days, when England herself was in the throes of a deadly struggle for the mastery of the sea, it must be allowed that Marryat's novels are unexceptionally sound in their moral tone.   Everywhere they are inspired by a manly independence, a love of virtue and truth, and a devotion to duty, while honour and courage are shown to be the priceless things they really are.   Although, too, Marryat is eminently sensational, as the phrase now runs, he never sinks into extravagances, and he does not dilate on horrors for the mere purpose of shocking the reader into the questionable pleasure of being revolted and sickened.

In *Peter Simple*, for example, there is an ample fund of the most healthy fun ; and what book of the kind is more manly in tone? This is the glory of Marryat. Look at any of his many novels— *The King's Own, Percival Keene, Jacob Faithful,* etc. —and in all we find the simple staple virtues of the *practical* Christian life are fully encouraged. Courage, truth, generosity and loyalty to all that is duty—these are the virtues inculcated by incidents and dialogue, as the latter is made to reveal the characters of the stories, and thence the net outcome of all Captain Marryat's books is that of a thoroughly healthy morality, wholly devoid of anything like preaching or bringing forward of aught like "a purpose" in the narrative.

Peter Simple, Jacob Faithful, and *The King's Own,* that fine novel containing a true account of the mutiny of the Nore, are probably among the best known of Marryat's novels; but there are many novels which are quite as good, or, in some respects, better even than these. *The Poacher* is a remarkable, rather introspective story, wherein the hero is a little boy (Joey Rushbrook) who witnesses his father, the poacher, shoot his enemy in the course of a violent quarrel, and heroically resolves to leave his home and parents, and go forth alone into the world, in order to divert suspicion from his father. The adventures of the boy are full of the greatest interest, including a sequence of striking incidents ingeniously worked

into the tissue of the main plot.   Here comes in
the comic bit about bombastic naval despatches,
wherein a fourteen-gun brig, happening to sail
right in among a fleet of chassemarés (coasting
luggers), frightened three into surrender, and sus-
tains herself no damage beyond a little chipping
from the only shot of a French shore battery that
fired on her.   The luggers are written of as "three-
masted vessels," the fire from the poor little
battery is magnified into a broadside engagement,
and although it could not be said that His
Majesty's ship had any killed, a long list of casualties
was made out, as it happened that a dozen of the
sailors, while hauling at a rope, fell back on the
deck, through a shot cutting the rope, and were, of
course, more or less bruised!   Then one man
scorched his hand at his gun, and another nearly
jammed his finger off!   The whole story is in
Marryat's best mock heroic style.   In the issue the
poacher (Joey's father) becomes a man of property,
and ultimately the murder comes to light; and the
self-sacrificing son, now a young man of great
promise, is charged with the crime.   It may
readily be imagined how very dramatic the story
then becomes.

The Naval Officer, or Frank Mildmay, is another
good novel, and includes an account of Trafalgar.
In Midshipman Easy we have a series of very

comic episodes, some of the incidents, as in that of a triangular duel, being conceived in the spirit of an outrageous but perfectly innocent fun.

Taken together these sea novels of Marryat's form a distinct epoch in English fiction, and they remain additions thereto, equally honourable and permanent. About contemporary with Captain Marryat was Captain Chamier, who likewise served with distinction at sea, and, retiring at the same time as Marryat, produced several nautical novels, of which the best are *Ben Brace*, *The Arethusa, Tom Bowling*, and some others. Chamier writes well, and in a practical manner. He fully understands his subject, and is decidedly worth reading ; but he is far below Marryat in literary force. Both these writers have, however, done much to inspire healthy English lads with a love of, and an interest in, the sea ; and from some obvious view-points it is certain that these novels, especially Marryat's, are really to be reckoned as belonging to the national side of imaginative literature. If in the case of Marryat we could only see a complete portrait gallery of all his distinct characters, British and foreign, the rich-ness of his resources, and the true dramatic spirit of his fine genius, would be abundantly apparent. How many and how real his characters are !

In this connection it is well to notice one writer

5

—an American—who has given us a sort of sea novel without a plot, but abounding in incidents and delineations of character. I allude to Richard Henry Dana, who wrote *Two Years before the Mast*, which is really a standard book. This applies, however, more especially to the American merchant service, and it has been reserved for Mr. Clark Russell to create as strong an interest, perhaps, in contemporary seafaring life as Marryat did in the men-of-war of his day. Mr. Russell is a thorough adept in all that appertains to the mercantile marine, and he has invoked the aid of romance, history and legend, to render his novels attractive, which they undoubtedly are. One of the latter deals with the legend of the Flying Dutchman, which, by the way, Marryat has wrought up into his novel of the *Phantom Ship*. Here the interest turns on the son of Vanderdecken, the Flying Dutchman himself, while his wife, a beautiful being, named Amine, falls into the hands of the Inquisition at Goa. But to revert, one of Mr. Clark Russell's representative novels is, perhaps, that entitled *Between the Forelands*. Here we have an account of some of the most moving and salient of the more historic events that have occurred in those familiar home-waters which flow between the North and South Forelands. These grand headlands have seen, indeed, much that is splendid and much that is disastrous in the marine annals of England. One of the great incidents in this book is the awful tragedy of the men-of-war shipwrecked on the fatal Goodwin Sands during the fearful storm of 1703.

One of Mr. Clark Russell's later sea novels is entitled the *Emigrant Ship*. The plot is simple enough : a sailing vessel bound for Australia, and having on board a number of female emigrants, loses, through a chapter of amusing accidents, the whole of her crew, excepting only the hero of the story, who is then thrown on his resources, and in the issue enlists some of the women as a new crew, attires them in seamanlike garb, and after many diverting incidents brings the ship safely to Sydney.

All these books are of a thoroughly healthy tone, and they may be regarded as among the type of what may be conveniently termed informatory fiction.

They are all more or less inspired by the spirit of William Motherwell's well-known lines—

Our eagle wings of might we stretch before the gallant
  wind,
And we leave the tame and sluggish earth a dim, mean
  speck behind ;
We shoot into the untracked deep as earth-freed spirits
  soar,
Like stars of fire through boundless space—through
  realms without a shore !

While, however, Marryat has given us in *Newton Forster* a very fair idea of the merchant service as it was, it has been reserved for American novelists to delineate the aspect of life before the mast in the mercantile marine down to our own days. I have spoken of Dana, and with him must be mentioned Herman Melville, an American novelist, and the son of a merchant, who, having a passion for the sea, embarked in a ship bound for London, when only eighteen, as a sailor before the mast. Mr. Melville met with many adventures ; he visited Tahiti, and eventually settled down to domestic life and literature. He is the author of *Typee*, an account of his very curious experiences in the Marquesas Islands; and among his other somewhat notable novels may be cited *Omoo, or Adventures in the South Seas*, wherein much is vividly delineated of the dusky beauties of the Pacific; while *Redburn* is a chapter in the life of a sailor, and *White Jacket* is another of his novels. Mr. Hume Nisbet has in the *Jolly Roger* produced a sea-story of Elizabethan days.

Then James Hannay (1827-1873) must not be forgotten, who served in the navy till 1845, and wrote one really nautical novel, *Singleton Fontenoy;* while two sea tales of Mr. Michael Scott still worthily survive in *Tom Cringle's Log* and the *Cruise of the "Midge"*.

Allusion has been made above to Clark Russell

(1844), the son of the famous composer and author of " Cheer, Boys, Cheer".

In many ways Mr. Russell is to the mercantile marine what Marryat was to the navy. His first nautical novel appeared in 1874, under the title of *John Holdsworth, Chief Mate*, and met with instant success. One of the most popular of his novels is the *Wreck of the "Grosvenor,"* wherein are in a measure anticipated the efforts subsequently made by Mr. Plimsoll to improve the dietary of British sailors. Among Mr. Clark Russell's principal novels may be mentioned *An Ocean Free Lance, The Frozen Pirate*, a singular and yet realistic fantasy, *My Shipmate Louise*, the *Romance of Jenny Marlowe*, and others.

I ought to mention that although Charles Reade is not exactly a nautical novelist, he has in one or two of his novels given some very stirring scenes of stress and storm at sea. Thus in *Hard Cash* an encounter occurs between a merchantman and some Chinese pirates, which is a fine piece of writing ; *Foul Play* is another sea story of Reade's.

There is here among the authors cited abundant choice for those who love to read of sailors and the sea. Year by year, as I said above, the world of many waters grows more populous, and doubtless, amid its increasing press and hurry of competitive life, new chroniclers will arise to charm us with its contemporary features, as Cooper and Marryat have done with those of the past.

CHAPTER VI

POLITICAL NOVELS.

FOR most of us politics, *per se*, are dry, except when their course happens to lie in the track that leads to stirring episodes, or even, it may be, to great disasters. Yet, usually, the political novel is found to be interesting, and from it many have drawn useful information that but for its help would never have been theirs. It is, however, by a cruel paradox, the fact that the novel that most faithfully reflects the politics of its day, is generally the most dull to a succeeding generation, whatever may be its value as a record.

Obviously the scope of the political novel is wide, and the writer must needs be versatile. An old poet says :—

> A politician—Protean-like—must alter
> His face and habit; and like water seem
> Of the same colour that the vessel is
> That doth contain it.

This implies for the novelist of political life a remarkable acquaintance with and a keen appreciation of the arts whereby men are influenced and governed. There can be no doubt that as a means for studying practical politics the novel offers many advantages to intelligent readers, who may gather thence much that otherwise would probably be never known to them, or, if known, not properly understood.

Probably one of the earliest writers of political novels was Robert Plumer Ward, himself an English statesman and in 1806 Under-Secretary of State for Foreign Affairs. He wrote three notable novels, *De Vere, Tremaine,* and *De Clifford.* In him we perceive, as is, indeed, the case with all good writers, that practical experience of actual life was worked up and fully utilised.

If we take quantity, it may be said that, on the whole, the most conspicuous political novelist is the late Lord Beaconsfield. In his fine novel *Sybil, or the Two Nations,* is a powerfully drawn and Rembrandt-like picture in many ways of the down-trodden industrial classes as they were early in the Victorian period. Then in others of his many novels are sketches more or less vivid of many of the notable statesmen of his time. Lord Beaconsfield, as Mr. Disraeli, was the leader of what was known as the Young England Party, wherein Conservatism was curiously combined with a very thorough form of Radicalism. Those who wish to study this should read *Coningsby*, *Sybil*, and *Tancred*, published 1844-47, wherein the principles of " Young England " are set forth.

The first Lord Lytton, who concentrated in himself so many types of the novelist, delineated in *My Novel*, one of his masterpieces, a very accurate view of English political life from the party standpoint, and gives the humours of an election for Parliament with much force.

Politics in England are in a great measure necessarily equivalent to party; and thence, as first one and then the other party comes uppermost, and, further, as parties often blend and borrow ideas and even policies from each other, there is in contemporary politics an absence of definite form and of finality debarring novelists in general from producing any very enduring work; for how can a base be found on the surging seas of our party government which, if good in itself, does not readily lend itself to the shaping hand of the literary artist ? If we contrast the earliest political novels of Lord Beaconsfield with his latest efforts, *Lothair* and *Endymion*, this fact is at once apparent.   Both these last-cited novels are remarkable; but, as we read, we are reminded constantly that these pages deal with things that are unstable and transitory. Some of these novels, indeed, clever as they are, resemble pamphlets expanded, the main arguments of which are delivered in dialogue from the lips of fairly well-drawn celebrities of the day, male and female after their kind; but while there is much of art there is little of nature, and but a modicum of true enthusiasm or genuine passion.

These political novels may be read with some profit. Far different is it with the political novels of the first Lord Lytton. He, like Disraeli, began as a Democrat, and ended, like Lord Beaconsfield, as a solid Conservative. Almost the first novel that the first Lord Lytton produced was political; for *Paul Clifford*, the work here referred to, is really an indictment of English law as it then existed and was administered in matters criminal. In this novel, one of the most witty of the Lytton fictions, is found a strong plea against capital punishment, and it enunciates, too, many revolutionary doctrines. This vein, alloyed with more reason and much rhetoric, is found also in *Rienzi*, a later and far more mature work, wherein forms of government, despotism, and popular liberty are ably discussed. Lord Lytton, indeed, closed his splendid career as a Conservative, and is in many ways a parallel to Lord Beaconsfield. It is also noticeable how much ripened wisdom is apparent in *Kenelm Chillingly*, one of the latest and best of the Lytton library of novels and romances. In this work is an ample fund of philosophy and disquisition on the politics of the day, and in the hero's utterances on Democracy v. Aristocracy, is much that is pointed and suggestive. In this delightful book will be found that loveliest of all the Lytton female creations, Lily Mordaunt, who tames butterflies and whose story is one of the most pathetic in all the Lytton literature. The novel is a rare and delicate mixture of the romantic and the real, the two being artfully blended in a beautiful atmosphere of true poetry. Lily marries one she does not love from a mistaken idea of duty—an ordinary incident, it will be said, in fiction ; but so delicately, so truthfully and so powerfully has the pathos of the sacrifice been wrought out, that few, indeed, can read the closing portion of this sweet sad episode without being moved to tears—such tears, in truth, as soften and humanise, rendering us all better through the purifying influence of sympathy. There are, indeed, in some of the Lytton novels passages which stand out in vivid beauty and true power as gems of English prose, impassioned by real feeling into genuine poetry.

Charles Kingsley, who as a popular clergyman did so much to popularise what is known as "muscular Christianity," was also a political novelist. He was, indeed, at one period known as the " Chartist Parson," and in his novel *Alton Locke* he eloquently vindicates the rights of the industrial classes. In *Alton Locke* will be found a vivid account of the great Chartist movement of 1848, when this country appeared on the very brink of a terrible social revolution. *Yeast* is another of Kingsley's political novels, touching on the game laws. Few writers knew better than Charles Kingsley the typical working man, or had a truer sympathy with his lot.

Mr. Edward Jenkins (1838) has written political fiction. His story *Ginx's Baby* met with phenomenal success. He is an advanced Liberal, and advocates imperial unity.

The late Mr. Froude, the historian, turning to fiction after writing history, has produced in the *Two Chiefs of Dunboy* a fine political novel, going to many of the roots of the Irish disaffection, recalling the days when the disaffected Irish looked to France for material aid against the hated Saxon.

The lines are somewhat stilted, but they may be aptly cited, wherein we are reminded that in reply to the question—What constitutes a State? it is not—

> Cities proud with spires and turrets crowned,
>   Nor bays and broad armed ports,
> Where, laughing at the storm, rich navies ride;

Nor starred nor spangled courts,
Where low-browed baseness wafts perfume to pride,
No! men, high-minded men.

Certainly, one of the many practical lessons to
be learned from the perusal of political novels is
the rarity of those whose only motive is the public
good.   The many political novels of Lord Beaconsfield, of the first Lord Lytton, and of others, go far
to demonstrate how prevailing a motor in public
action is simple selfishness.   Here, as generally in
the rational reading of wisely chosen novels, more
may and should be learned than can ever be
gathered from the newspapers, or even, perhaps,
from personal participation in the turmoil of actual
public life.

One of the latest examples of the political novel
up to date, to adopt the current phrase of the late
nineteenth century, is the work entitled *When We
were Boys*, written in prison by Mr. William O'Brien,
a prominent member of the Parnellite Party, and
the editor of *United Ireland*.   Mr. O'Brien, being
imprisoned under the Coercion Act, beguiled the
tedium of captivity by composing a novel which is
of considerable length and full of characteristic
Irish touches.   It is also full of rebels, as may be
well imagined, and one scene represents the finding
of a secreted rebel banner in the centre of which

gleam the beams of a rising sun, the sunburst of the rebel flag!

Mr. Justin McCarthy, another M.P., is also a political novel writer, and has produced the *Rebel Rose* and the *Ladies' Gallery*.

CHAPTER VII

SCOTCH AND IRISH NOVELS.

NEAR to, or at the root of, most of the manly virtues lies patriotism. It is found in all robust natures rather as an instinct than a principle, and it is to very many a true passion. This is, doubtless, the reason why national literature remains so popular, notwithstanding the influence of the growing cosmopolitan spirit of the day.

Every one agrees that of North Britain, from the patriotic point of view, the representative novelist is Sir Walter Scott, who remains pre-eminently first. He towers high above all others, and though much of his work has been described as that of the improvisatore, all in all, where can we find in prose fiction his parallel ?

Much of the fame of Scott rests securely on his Scottish novels. In *Guy Mannering, Old Mortality,* the *Black Dwarf, Rob Roy,* and *A Legend of Montrose,* with its Dugald Dalgety, one of the best portraits of a soldier of fortune in British fiction, we have a marvellous collection of patriotic novels.

But to these must be added the *Heart of Midlothian*, *Waverley*, and the *Fair Maid of Perth*. All these works show Scott to be an eminently national novelist. It has been said that he is only objective in his work. This is the verdict of admirers of the more analytical subjective writers, who require many pages of subtle reasoning to show what Scott, like Shakespeare, often gives in a suggestive sentence or a scrap of dialogue that sounds like real speech. Then, too, let it be borne in mind that the successful objective writer practically includes the subjective element, for he gives us flesh and blood creatures, and the reader soon imagines the rest about any fictitious portraitures that are presented with true realism ; whereas often the subjective writer gives simply his own abstractions, run into a verbal mould, which only simulates something that would serve just as well for the inner evolutions of some other subjective novelist. But Scott could be subjective too. Let us take the *Fair Maid of Perth*. That novel gives first of all the best picture extant of the High-landers of Scotland in feudal days ; and in the character of Conachar, or, as he becomes late in the story, Ian Eachin Mac Ian, son of the chief of the clan Quhele, we have the high-water mark of Scott's dramatic power. Here, be it noted, we have an analysis of character, and an example of

Scott in a subjective aspect. Conachar is a constitutional coward, but all the same he possessed the pride of his high lineage, and the struggle in his soul when he is called on to prove that he has physical courage, wherein he is utterly wanting, is unquestionably both conceived and executed on the Shakespearian plane of true dramatic art.

Turn now to the other characters in this magnificent novel of varied character and incident, of lively dialogue and of introspective musings, of comedy and farce, as in the ridiculous adventures of the poltroon Oliver Proudfute with Devil's Dick of Hellgarth, and see how rich it is. Throughout told with a supreme force, the narrative deepens at length into the intense pathos of the terrible fate of the Duke of Rothsay, and into the sombre Greek-like tragedy of the despairing Conachar. Here we have, too, the frank, faithful, genial smith fighting for his own hand, the old unhappy king, his intriguing nobles, all dramatically discriminated and delineated in Scott's most masterly manner.

All the female characters are admirable. Then there is the original conception of Dwining, the poisoner, while Ramorny, the profligate but ambitious noble of the time, is a type of character that stands forth distinct among the masterpieces of fiction.

Besides the great head of the school of patriotic

and national fiction, there are many who have achieved distinction, and who will well repay perusal.

Let us turn to John Gibson Lockhart (1774-1854), who married Scott's eldest daughter, and wrote the famous life of the great novelist.   Lockhart produced two or three notable novels—*Adam Blair*, a story of Scottish life, *Reginald Dalton*, and *Valerius*.   This last is a study of Roman life.

John Wilson (1785-1854), better known to some as " Christopher North," produced some eminently national novels.   Like Thackeray he lost a fortune in early life, and was thus driven to literature, wherein he achieved much success in various departments.   In his *Margaret Lyndsay* there will be found a tender idyllic grace, and his *Lights and Shadows of Scottish Life* shed much light on the times to which they refer.

More gifted for fiction than either Lockhart or Wilson, is John Galt (1779-1839), who in 1804, panting for literary fame, came to London with an epic poem on the battle of Largs, which did not find acceptance.   After the usual vicissitudes, Galt succeeded in prose fiction, and his novels, the *Annals of the Parish, Sir Andrew Wylie*, the *Entail*, the *Ayrshire Legatees*, and *Ringan Gilhaize*, a tale of the Scottish Covenanters, abound in stirring scenes and powerful delineations of

6

national character. Galt, indeed, showed the
way to a school of novelists familiar enough now.
He is a master of the art of reproducing pro-
vincial scenes, and in faithfully portraying life as
it actually was in the old Scottish communities
where even the small shopkeeper might, and sometimes did, come to be chief magistrate. One of
his best novels is the *Provost*.

Among North British novelists we must not
overlook Susan Ferrier (1782-1854), who was a
special friend and a literary favourite of the great
Sir Walter. In her youth, Miss Ferrier saw much
of Scottish society at its best, and reproduced, in
her novels *Marriage*, the *Inheritance*, and *Destiny,
or the Chief's Daughter*, much of the life she had
actually seen. These novels are all marked by
wit, a keen appreciation of the comic side of life,
and generally we find in them a highly sympathetic reproduction of the peculiarities of the
dwellers north of the Tweed.

James Hogg (1772-1835), the Ettrick Shepherd
and poet, wrote many novels. The best of these
are, perhaps, the *Brownie of Bodsbeck*, the *Three
Perils of Man*, the *Three Perils of Woman*, and the
Altrive Tales.

Another distinguished novelist is William Black
(1841), author of *Macleod of Dare*, *In Far Lochaber*,
and the *Strange Adventures of a Phaeton*. Mr.

Black has written many novels, too, not related to Scottish life *per se*. His novel *In Silk Attire* gives much space to a description of peasant life in the Black Forest. Among Mr. Black's novels are *A Daughter of Heth, A Princess of Thule, Judith Shakespeare,* and many others. In regard to the latter work and some others wherein Shakespeare is made to appear, one always wishes that the co-operation of a Walter Savage Landor could have been secured.

Robert Buchanan (1841) is a Scottish novelist and poet, but in most of his novels the scene is laid out of North Britain. Among his novels are the *Martyrdom of Madeline,* the *Shadow of the Sword,* and *Foxglove Manor.*

Another poet novelist is George Macdonald (1824), who is an idealist, and at times a mystic. He is deeply imbued with true religious feeling. Among his chief works are *Robert Falconer, David Elginbrod, Alec Forbes of Howglen, Annals of a Quiet Neighbourhood,* the *Seaboard Parish, Malcolm,* and many others. He is at times a clear and practical thinker, but on occasions he can lead his readers delightedly forth into the nebulous realms of metaphysics, illumined, however, by the rainbow glow of a true poetic fancy.

A special exponent of Scottish life, especially in its domestic phase, is Mr. J. M. Barrie (1860), who struck a firm note in *Auld Licht Idylls,* and achieved marked distinction by his stories entitled *A Window in Thrums,* and the *Little Minister.* He is the author, too, of *When a Man's Single.*

Before leaving Scotland, it may be well to mention that, without Scott, we may read a complete course of North British history by taking a series of Scottish novels and romances, beginning with the thirteenth century. Thus, *Sir Michael Scott,* by A. Cunningham, starts the course; the *Days of Bruce* (G. Aguilar); the *Caged Lion* (captivity of James I.), by C. M. Yonge; *Days of Yore,* by S. Tytler; the *Braes of Yarrow* (times of James V.), by C. Gibbon; *Mary of Lorraine* (battle of Pinkie), by James Grant; *Bothwell* (Mary Queen of Scots), same author; *Magdalen Hepburn,* by Mrs. Oliphant; the *Queen's Maries,* by Whyte Melville; *Tales of the Wars of Montrose,* by James Hogg; the *Adventures of Rob Roy,* by James Grant; and in the *White Cockade,* by the same author, is set forth the story of the fight at Falkirk and that of fatal Culloden.

Let us now glance at the more distinctive novelists of the sister kingdom. How evanescent is fame! Probably few young readers now know much of John Banim (1800-1842); yet he was regarded as being to Ireland what Scott is to Scotland. Among his best novels are the first and second series of the *Tales of the O'Hara Family.* Banim produced a number of tales of Irish life, wherein is much virility, and a real power of depicting traits of national character. The *Denounced*, and several others, are good solid works, based largely on the best results of personal observation. As a delineator of the old Irish peasant, Banim has few rivals.

Samuel Lover (1797-1868) was also once one of the leading Irish novelists. *Rory O'More*, a romance of Irish life, won great popularity; and among his more distinctive works are *Treasure Trove, Handy Andy*, and others.

Maturin, already alluded to under another section, wrote, under the title of *Eva*, a novel dealing with the English invasion under Strongbow.

Then there is William Carleton (1798-1869), who in a lighter vein is a very skilful delineator of the special traits of the Irish. Among his novels are the *Black Prophet*, graphically describing the appalling features of the famine of 1846, and *Rody the Rover*, the *Tithe Proctor*, and especially the *Traits and Stories of the Irish Peasantry*, not forgetting his more popular work *Willy Reilly*. Carleton wrote the *Misfortunes of Barney Branagan, Valentine McClutchy*, a defence of the Irish Catholic priests, and a plea for separation from England; and it is certain that under the guise of fiction Carleton is a sympathetic historian of the Irish people.

Gerald Griffin (1803-1840) was once a popular Irish novelist. His *Collegians* was dramatised, and, as the *Colleen Bawn*, holds the British stage; and mention should be made of his *Tales of the Munster Festivals*.

Mrs. Anna Maria Hall (1808-1881) produced in 1828 her *Sketches of Irish Character;* and this was followed by the *Buccaneers*, wherein Cromwell appears. Among her best known novels are the *Whiteboy* and *Stories of the Irish Peasantry*.

Miss Edgeworth (1767-1849) wrote some distinctively Irish novels. She was of Irish parentage, but educated in England. In 1801 she put forth *Castle Rack Rent*, which immediately stamped her as a capable exponent of native Irish peculiarities. Several of her novels were written expressly to show some special phases of Irish life, and also to set forth some grievances, as in the case of the *Absentee*.

Lever (1809-1872), mentioned elsewhere, is an Irish novelist, and in many of his fine and racy delineations has achieved a wondrous verisimilitude, more particularly in showing the more volatile phases of Celtic character.

Reference should be made to Lady Blessington's *Grace Cassidy*, and to Lady Duff Gordon's *Stella and Vanessa*, a story of the days of Dean Swift. Then, besides the late Mr. Froude's *Two Chiefs of*

Dunboy, and Mr. W. O'Brien's *When We were Boys*, there is Mr. Justin McCarthy (1830), who has written *A Fair Saxon*, and many other charming novels.

Chapter VIII.

COMIC AND HUMOROUS NOVELS.

LAUGHTER, confined within due bounds, is peptic;
it helps the whole internal economy of man and
woman to work properly, and it softens and dis-
solves, as in a golden crucible, all petty cares,
rankling jealousies, and the uncharitableness of life.

In one word, fun is a fine solvent for all un-
wholesome humours; and thence it is no doubt
that we all feel such sincere gratitude to the man
who really amuses us.

Well, indeed, has Francis Beaumont, that fine
old dramatist, declared that—

'Tis mirth that fills the veins with blood,
More than wine, or sleep or food;
Let each man keep his heart at ease;
No man dies of that disease.
He that would his body keep
From diseases must not weep;
But whoever laughs and sings,
Never he his body brings
Into fevers, gouts, or rheums,
Or lingeringly his lungs consumes;
But contented lives for aye :
The more he laughs the more he may.

COMIC AND HUMOROUS NOVELS.

There are, no doubt, in English fiction more writers who move us to tears than those who impel us to laugh. Mirth, genuine and thorough, has not greatly permeated English fiction as yet, and our humorists are often of—

> That nature that does make
> One's fancy chuckle, while his heart does ache.

Like the clown, the jester is soon forgotten. It is in the very nature of things that he should pass away with those whom he has amused and tickled. The fictionist who takes life as a good joke, necessarily dallies with the surface and with what is evanescent, and is the chronicler of the fashions of the hour. We who come after that fashion has long departed, often fail to perceive where the fun was. The surfaces of social life are ever changing, and one generation knows little of the wit of another.

The one great exception to this principle is found doubtless in Charles Dickens, who to many doubtless seems the very creator of the comic novel, although, as I shall show, this is not exactly the case. Before, however, dealing with Dickens we must turn to the first great master of humorous English fiction—Laurence Sterne—who is doubtless from some view-points the greatest of all English humorists who have made fiction its special vehicle. He was born at Clonmel, Ireland, in

1713.   His father, a lieutenant in a marching regiment, led a very wandering life, and at the age of ten the boy was sent to a relative, Mr. Sterne, of Elvington, Yorkshire.   In due course Laurence Sterne went to Cambridge and graduated, selecting the Church as his vocation.   He obtained a Yorkshire living, married, and for twenty years was unheard of by the world.   There is reason to believe that the greater part of his time went in reading, painting, and playing the violin and shooting.   It was not until 1759, when he published the first two volumes of *Tristram Shandy*, that he became, like Byron, famous in a day.   On going to London he was welcomed as a veritable literary lion.   More volumes of *Tristram Shandy* appeared, succeeded by the *Sentimental Journey*; and in 1768 Sterne died, having practically given up his clerical duties for the dissipations of the life of a literary celebrity. *Tristram Shandy* is his one great work.   Captain Shandy is the hero of the novel : he is represented as being benevolent, generous and brave, but simple as a child.   It has been said that *Tristram Shandy* will live as long as the English language because of its three characters—Old Shandy, Uncle Toby, and Corporal Trim.   These three may be well regarded as real creations.   They exhibit, indeed, a wonderful exuberance of fancy; and even the long digressions wherewith the work abounds, are full of whimsical humour. In some passages, too, Sterne shows himself undoubtedly a master of pathos.

Before quitting the eighteenth century, some allusion should be made to Thomas Amory (1691-1788), an eccentric and humorous English author. At one time his distinctive work, in four volumes, the *Life of John Buncle, Esq.*, was popular; John Buncle is described as a "prodigious hand at matrimony, divinity, and a song". He is also stated to have married seven women, and to have been widowed seven times. After each bereavement, he is described as being inconsolable, but, soon becoming resigned, marries again. The book is curious as showing the kind of thing that some of our forefathers revelled in as being altogether exquisite in its fun and humour.

We now turn to Charles Dickens. It is certain that Dickens, like many other great writers, did not at first know where his real strength lay. He began his career as a novelist with a purpose, *viz.*, that of exposing the real character of thieves. He had observed that generally what related to criminal life in literature had been invested with a strong flavour of fun or a glamour of romance. In *Oliver Twist* he sought to reproduce the realities of criminal life, and he decidedly succeeded as a realist, quite on the Zola plane, in his sketches of

Fagan, the "fence," and his school of young thieves. This was, of course, a great revulsion from Captain Macheath of the *Beggar's Opera,* that clever but mischievous work of Gay. It was quite different, too, from Dick Turpin, Jack Sheppard, and other low-life "heroes" of vice and violence, of whom Harrison Ainsworth produced an ample stock. Scott, however, did something of the same kind; and the scoundrels in the *Fortunes of Nigel* and some other of his romances are to the full as repulsive as Bill Sykes. Dickens, however, when penning the preface to *Oliver Twist,* shut his eyes to that, as he set forth what he believed to be his own particular literary mission. Even in *Oliver Twist,* however, we can readily discern touches of true humour when the "purpose" is temporarily dropped; and then we have flashes from the vast resources of wit and fun, which had just been poured forth so lavishly in the most comic of all British novels—*Pickwick.*

Dickens changed to a great extent the direction of comic and humorous fiction, and indeed completely revolutionised it. He soared so high above all his contemporaries, and, after the publication of *Pick-wick,* was so universally recognised as the amusing novelist, that something akin to an injustice—inevitable under the circumstances—was meted out to other writers, who, inferior to him on the whole, were still, in many cases, men of worth and mark, and were recognised by our forefathers as such.

Thus Samuel Warren (1807-1870), in his *Ten Thousand a Year*, gives unquestionably funny delineations of his vulgar hero Titmouse, who from the lowly estate of a draper's assistant, one of the most coarse and common type too, is elevated to an estate of ten thousand a year. He marries a peer's daughter and enters parliament. The greater portion of this novel is caricature, veined with satire and lighted by the glare of broad farce. But in the delineation of the true English gentleman and his family, whom Titmouse ejects from the estate he usurps for a time, Warren certainly shows powers of a high order; and here and there in this novel, over which our fathers roared with laughter, are evidences of the capacity for sounding well the deeper notes of genuine passion.

Henry Cockton, working on a far lower plane of art, produced in *Valentine Vox* an essentially laughable novel. But veiled under its fun and humour was a determined and a righteous onslaught on the abominable private lunatic asylums of those days; and in this he was paralleled by Charles Reade himself, who, in his powerful romance, *Hard Cash*, denounces the same evil.

Albert Smith (1816-1860), he of Mont Blanc fame, wrote several more or less comic novels, as the *Adventures of Mr. Ledbury, Christopher Tadpole,* and the *Scattergood Family,* and one melodramatic romance, the *Marchioness of Brinvilliers.* Though these works are now little known and less read they were in their day successful enough. Each period has its favourite laughter-provoking books, and only here and there do we find a writer standing pre-eminent as *the* laughter-making man of the day. As human life is necessarily travelling on to what promises to be at last its mental finalities in certain directions, it is impossible to safely predict to what the comic novel may come.

A very notable comic novel in its own peculiar vein was the *Adventures of Mr. Verdant Green,* by "Cuthbert Bede". This was the pen-name chosen by the Rev. Edward Bradley (1827-1889), who in this story gives a very realistic account of life at Oxford as it was many years ago. The book abounds in descriptions of practical jokes, and the humours of the university among fast men are cleverly drawn. This book achieved in its day enormous success.

Mr. Bradley, it is worthy of mention, was member of a family who have been clergymen with scarcely a break for three centuries. He graduated at Durham, and besides his typical novel, *Verdant Green,* he contributed to *Punch,* the *Illustrated London News,* etc.

Among living comic, humorous, and fanciful writers, is Mr. Thomas Anstey Guthrie (1856), who in *Vice Versâ* (1882) achieved extraordinary success. In this very remarkable effort of fancy, the fun depends on the absurd conception of a father who changes places with his little boy, he returning to school under the outward appearance of the lad, and the latter assuming the father's place ! Among other works from the same writer are the *Giant's Robe*, the *Black Poodle*, the *Tinted Venus*, and the *Pariah*. " Mr. Anstey," for that is the name under which Mr. Guthrie writes, does not, however, any more than Dickens, confine himself entirely to the comic element. The *Giant's Robe*, for instance, is the story of a man who pretends to have written a great book composed by his friend, who is supposed to be dead ; and here some of the fun arises out of the fact that the impostor does not understand properly the deeper portions of the book he pretends to have been written by himself.

Mr. B. L. Farjeon has lately published a curious novel entitled *Something Occurred,* wherein a young married couple, devotedly attached to each other, get into financial difficulties, and are extricated thence in a semi-supernatural manner, which results in the head of each being transferred to the other ! Mr. Farjeon is more fully dealt with under "Australian Novels ".

Douglas Jerrold (1803-1857), the famous wit, wrote several novels, one—the *Man Made of Money* —being a fanciful flight in somewhat the same direction wherein Mr. Anstey has achieved such popularity; Mr. Anstey, by the way, produced in 1894, under the title of *Under the Rose*, a story in scenes, wherein there is much satire and a good deal of mystification arising out of mistaken identity.

The comic or purely humorous novel is not very largely represented as yet in British fiction, although a very great many British novelists have infused into much of their fiction marked veins of the comic side of things.

Theodore Hook may be said to have produced a comic novel in *Jack Brag*, wherein a London tallow-chandler apes the gentleman, and has a series of unpleasant adventures until in the end he is completely exposed. The Brothers Mayhew, Henry, Horace, and Augustus, between 1846 and 1851, produced some funny fiction, including the *Greatest Plague in Life, or the Adventures of a Lady in Search of a Servant*, the *Image of his Father*, and some others. These, however, though much read at the time, are far from what would now be deemed good in a literary sense.

The writer has not yet arisen who comes quite level with Charles Dickens at his best ; and yet doubtless the present age is one which would

immediately welcome and richly reward the man
who could really raise at will hearty laughter.

Innocent laughter is not only the palpable
manifestation of joy, but it is the most healthful
of the bodily movements from some physiological
aspect. It greatly improves the digestion and the
whole circulation, and especially does it invariably
quicken the vital forces.

Aptly, indeed, an old writer has observed :—

> The greatness that would make us grave
>   Is but an empty thing;
> What more than mirth would mortals have ?
>   The happy man's a king !

It all depends, however, on what kind of mirth
is here meant.

The very worst thing about much of our literary
humour, wit, and fun is, beyond all dispute, its
rapidly increasing flippancy and its engrained
irreverence. It has been said—harsh as the saying must sound—that the one truly original
product of Transatlantic soil is the gross irreverence and unspeakable profanity of its humour.
This evil taint is creeping in among us through
the enormous growth of the periodical press; and
not a few of our novel writers exhibit a strong
tendency towards reproducing the most revolting
traits of American humour. Yet how good is
genuine humour ! A writer has said that the

7

union of true humour with sincere piety, guided by a just judgment, must be reckoned among the rarest manifestations of intellectual power.

No doubt a considerable bulk of the fiction of the day has nothing really cheerful about it. New endeavours are ever being made, as we are all aware, to import fresh forms of realism into the contemporary novel; but where shall we look for fun, fun such as bubbled up and ran over in laughter, in almost every page of *Pickwick*? When Mr. George Gissing introduces us to the people, the people of merrie England, at play, he transports us to the Crystal Palace, and depicts, as in the *Nether World*, the vagaries of a wedding party, from the unlovely purlieus of Clerkenwell; and the leading jester finds his wit runs in the fancy of grovelling down on the dusty floor of the Palace, for the purpose, it may be presumed, of tripping up the more unwary members of the party, whose sole idea of enjoyment is eating, drinking, and shouting, with the variation of shrieks and sounding slaps in the face from the females who in this manner endeavour to keep their cavaliers in some approximation to decent behaviour.

Never indeed was the agency of a really cheerful literature in fiction more needed, perhaps, than · in these pessimistic high-pressure feverish days. But, unfortunately, a great portion of the so-called cheerful literature of the hour is merely flippant, and in many instances extremely vicious. To deride, to decry, to belittle what is essentially noble, lofty, pure, and righteous, was not the way with the wits of the days of Sydney Smith, of Theodore Hook, and of Douglas Jerrold. Note how a gentle and playful wit plays about the pages of many of the early nineteenth-century novelists, and note how conspicuously this is the case in Sir Walter Scott. How much of it brightens the pages of the *Antiquary*, and how it relieves the deep-toned passion and the fearful tragedy of the *Bride of Lammermoor!* Was it not Sydney Smith who said that wit was a kind of inexplicable visitation, coming and going swiftly as lightning? And then glance at the amusing things put forth by the first Tom Hood. Who ever was the worse for any of them? Yet, as a latter nineteenth-century substitute, we have horseplay, practical joking, hurting or perhaps injuring somebody; and when this occurs, the readers are expected to be most diverted; while for art it is reckoned as exquisite fooling to scatter over pages of laboured but more or less feeble though flippant fun, drawings of a battered hat or a down-at-heel shoe or the like, —vagaries of the so-called "comic" art which our forefathers would have simply scouted as being beneath contempt. Little thought Leigh Hunt,

when he wrote his *Poetry of Wit and Humour,*
what it would come to through the vaunted
agency of the mighty latter nineteenth-century
pen and pencil.

In the estimation of very many, the great
humorist novelist of the day is J. M. Barrie, born
May 9, 1860, at Kirriemuir, a small town in For-
farshire. Mr. Barrie graduated as an M.A. at
Edinburgh in 1882, and then entered into active
journalistic work. His initial book, entitled *Better
Dead,* was simply a satire on life in London. Then
came a series of books each of which gained increased popularity, although it is, from a right view
of the novelist's art, rather a stretch to include
more than one or two as novels. It is curious, too,
to observe that the two specially distinctive of Mr.
Barrie's works scarcely contain more than 80 pages;
the stories in question—if stories they be—are *Auld
Licht Idylls* and *A Window in Thrums.* An admirer
of Mr. Barrie has said that *Auld Licht Idylls* is
practically an introduction to the whole series of Mr.
Barrie's works. It must be confessed that with
Mr. Barrie the story, however, is hardly the main
thing. In the novel curiously entitled *When a Man's
Single,* we have really a sketch of the literary life
struggle of a young man in London. The hero is
Rob Angus, originally a sawyer of Thrums, with a
decided literary bent. As a consequence he migrates

to the Midlands, and eventually makes his way to London, where he goes through terrible trials, and in the issue is rewarded with an income of £800 a year, as leader writer on a daily; and moreover, as is fitting in fiction, marries the lady of his choice. In this novel is a sketch of a kind of Bohemian journalist, who is certainly original; but of plots in the old-fashioned sense of the term there is little or none. The *Little Minister* is a finer work by far; but even here the plot is by no means of absorbing interest, and the writing is the main feature. Any way, Mr. Barrie has been enrolled among the new humorists; and in this connection mention must be made of the very amusing *jeu d'esprit*, *My Lady Nicotine*, wherein we have a highly diverting account of a man who is compelled to renounce his pipe and his bachelor friends in order to win the favour of the lady of his heart.

Charles Shirley Brooks was educated, like so many literary men, for the law, but abandoned it for journalism. He produced some amusing dramatic pieces, one of which, *Our New Governess*, was very funny, and finally wrote several novels, of which *Aspen Court*, the *Gordian Knot*, and the *Silver Cord* may be mentioned. He was a copious contributor to *Punch*.

Mark Lemon is mainly known as a writer of sparkling dramatic pieces, and as the editor of

Punch.   He is the author of two novels, however, each in three volumes, entitled *Wait for the End,* and *Loved at Last.*

One of the recognised exponents of the new school of humour is Mr. Jerome K. Jerome, who made a decided hit at first with his *Three Men in a Boat to Say Nothing of the Dog.*   Mr. Jerome's latest work is *John Ingerfield,* and other stories.

One of the latest types of novels marked by dry humour and a refined irony, is *Mr. Bailey-Martin,* by Percy White.   This is really the history, both introspective and objective, of a representative snob of the latter nineteenth century.   The society sketches are exceedingly well rendered; and the absence of exaggeration has rendered this an eminently interesting and amusing dissection of some of the special meannesses of human nature which seem to be the particular product of our high-pressure and complex civilisation.

Parallel in some sense to avowedly comic and humorous novels are parodies of serious fiction, of which the number has much increased of late years.   By "serious fiction" is meant, of course, every type of novel whose aim and end—however much it may amuse—is not necessarily to excite a laugh.   Parodies are very ancient, as the derivation of the word from the Greek *para*, beside, and *ode*, a song, indicates.   It is said that Greece invented the parody, and one of the earliest subjects thereof was Homer himself. The *Batrachomyoma-chia* (Battle of the Frogs and Mice) is one of the most ancient parodies, and has been erroneously ascribed to Homer himself. Among the Romans this species of literature distinctly marks the period of the decline of the empire. Poetry has naturally been exceedingly susceptible to the art of the parodist; but in prose fiction the two most notable examples of parodies thereon are furnished by two novelists, one English and one American, the former being one of our greatest—Thackeray —who, in his *Miscellanies*, gives some bright and clever parodies on sundry of his brother-novelists. In the case of Thackeray the parodies first appeared in *Punch*, entitled *Novels by Eminent Hands*, a series of burlesques on the works of Bulwer Lytton, "Harry Lorrequer" (Lever), G. P. R. James, and B. Disraeli. The parody on Disraeli appeared in 1847. It was entitled *Codlingsby*, by B. de Shrewsbury, and opened thus: "The noise in the old town was terrific; great Tom was booming sullenly over the uproar; the bell of Saint Mary's was clanging . . . groans of wounded men, cries of frightened females, cheers of either contending party proclaimed that the battle was at its height. In Berlin they would have said it was a revolution, and the cuirassiers would have been charging, sabre in hand, amidst that infuriate mob. In Cowbridge nobody heeded the disturbance—it was a town and gown row." Better known to the present generation than Thackeray's parodies on fiction, which are very entertaining in their satiric gambols, are the *Sensation Novels* of "Bret Harte," wherein the leading peculiarities of Dickens, Scott, Cooper, Hawthorne, Marryat, Thackeray himself, and others, are very cleverly hit off. The following extract is certainly a very exact reproduction of the style and also the mannerism of Dickens : "Don't tell me that it wasn't a knocker. I had seen it often enough, and ought to know. So ought the three o'clock beer, in dirty highlows, swinging himself over the railings, or executing a demoniacal jig on the door step. . . . So ought the postman, to whom knockers of the most extravagant were merely human weaknesses, that were to be pitied and used "—and so on. One of the best parodies of "Bret Harte's" is that on Disraeli's *Lothair*, the novel for which the author, then Lord Beaconsfield, received the very remarkable price of £10,000. Here is a specimen : "'Mamma, I've just dropped a pearl,' said the lady Coriander, bending over the Persian hearth-rug. 'From your lips, sweet friend?' said Lothaw, who came of age and entered the room at the same moment. 'No, from my work. It was a very valuable

pearl, mamma; papa gave Isaacs and Sons £50,000
for the two.' 'Ah, indeed,' said the duchess,
languidly rising; 'let us go to luncheon.' 'But,
your grace,' interposed Lothaw, who was still quite
young and had dropped on all fours on the carpet
in search of the missing gem, ' consider the value.'
' Dear friend,' interposed the duchess with infinite
tact, gently lifting him by the tails of his dress-
coat, ' I am waiting for your arm.' " More pointed,
perhaps, is " Bret Harte's " parody, *Mr. Midshipman Breezy*, aimed at Captain Marryat's truly
farcical novel *Midshipman Easy*. The opening
is characteristic of the style of the great naval
novelist in getting his story launched. " My
father was a north-country surgeon. He had
retired, a widower, from Her Majesty's navy many
years before, and had a small practice in his native
village. When I was seven years old, he employed
me to carry medicines to his patients. Being of
a lively disposition, I sometimes amused myself
during my daily rounds by mixing the contents of
the different phials. Although I had no reason to
doubt that the general result of this practice was
beneficial, yet as the death of a consumptive curate
followed the addition of a strong mercurial lotion
to his expectorant, my father concluded to with-
draw me from the profession and send me to
school."

Many other examples might be cited. "Ouida" especially, and Miss Braddon, are both very open to burlesque, as in the parody on *Lady Aurorabella* (*Aurora Floyd*), who is described at the opening as having received news that, in spite of all her homicidal exertions, her five husbands are again at liberty. This parody, by the way, is by Mr. Walter Parke. In regard to the first Lord Lytton (Edward Bulwer Lytton), perhaps one of the most pointed of Thackeray's parodies was that entitled *George de Barnwell*, wherein a thief and a murderer is elevated into a hero after the manner of *Eugene Aram*, a novel wherein the first Lord Lytton has worked up in an adroit manner a vast quantity of false sentiment. Parodies will always remain popular among certain classes of readers; and one of the best collections is that collected and published in six volumes by Mr. Walter Hamilton.

It is well, however, to warn the reader, that in general literature no taste is so perilous to the mind and character as that for parody. It is a taste that grows intense by over-indulgence, and in excess it ends by becoming rather a curse than a recreation. It was Hogarth himself, that master of caricature, who, in his latter days, lamented bitterly the fell effect of his own genius for artistic parodying; and declared that it had quite destroyed for him all pleasure in things beautiful, lovely and exalted.

Moderation, doubtless, is the sole secret for per-
petuating all enjoyment ; and certainly moderation
in parody reading is essential for those who do
not desire to have their nobler faculties for the
appreciation of the good and the beautiful, the true
and the pure, sapped away by slow degrees and
ultimately destroyed.   Laughter unquestionably is
a good and a very healthy function, and by all
means let it be indulged to the full ; but then it is
infinitely better to stimulate this faculty through
the medium of avowedly comic and humorous
novels, of which there are enough and to spare in
these days, rather than to cultivate the perilous
taste for caricature which commences with things
harmless enough, and producing at first simply fun,
may all too readily glide into a confirmed taste
which eventually can make only a mockery and a
jest of things and thoughts which should remain
for ever unspeakably sacred.

CHAPTER IX

SENSATIONAL NOVELS.

FROM one point of view every novel, in order to make any impression on readers, must be, to some extent, sensational. Otherwise it will be flat indeed. But, as we all know, a special significance attaches to the word when applied to novels; and it means briefly that the novelists in these cases employ altogether extraordinary agencies for compelling the reader's attention. In all of us are organs of curiosity and of wonder; and these, when once really roused, carry us away for a time into a charmed region, where the mind in reality is rather fascinated than exercised.

There are two special types of true sensational novels which claim attention here. The one owes little of its charm, such as it is, to any sort of art, properly so called; and the literary workmanship is of the lowest order, comprehending little beyond grammar and perspicuity. These work and act on readers exactly like newspaper reports of appalling catastrophes and horrible crimes, and are read from precisely the same motives. This is obviously the novel sensational in its perfectly raw or crude state ; and when once skimmed over, it is cast aside exactly like the evening paper with the latest telegram. Such works as these do not really, in any proper sense of the word, belong to literature, and need no further remark here. The other type of sensational novel is very different indeed, and includes sometimes great novels whereto have been superadded extraordinary and overwhelming incidents, as, say, in the *Last Days of Pompeii*, wherein sensation succeeds sensation, until the whole culminates in one overpowering horror of despair and doom.

During certain periods in our literary history, no doubt, sensational novels have been practically unknown, and the contemporary novelist has been compelled to keep within certain well-defined limits. Thus, at one time, it was an unwritten law of fiction that the hero of the orthodox novel must never be subject to any kind of physical infirmity. Nothing beyond a headache, or possibly a slight giddiness, was permitted ; and the bare notion of what is now familiar enough in the way of disease or aught physiological as a mainspring of action, would have been met then with a scream of horror. Yet, during all these periods, it must be confessed that the sensational novel lay in abeyance simply as a thing out of fashion rather than one unknown. For its genesis carries us back to the days of William Godwin, who, in *Caleb Williams*, produced what may, perhaps, be justly called the first truly artistic sensational novel. In this powerful work the hero, Falkland, a man of refinement and fortune, is repeatedly and grossly insulted by a coarse-minded territorial magnate, named Tyrrel, his social equal, but in all ways his intellectual inferior. Falkland at last, goaded to madness, assassinates his enemy, and then most ingeniously fastens the crime on his servant Caleb Williams, who has to fly, and finds himself pursued by the unrelenting hate of his guilty master, who seeks to immolate Williams in order to preserve his own honour unstained before the world. Caleb passes through many fearful trials, and goes for years in daily terror of arrest. All this is wrought up with consummate skill and admirable art ; and so human-like are the principal characters, that the reader feels sympathy for most of them, even for the arch-villain himself— a sure sign of the verisimilitude of the fiction.

I may pause to interpolate the remark that as a convenient and clear distinction it may be fairly held that what really constitutes the true sensational novel is crime in some form or other. In a word, something criminal must underlie and influence the action, and impart a determining tinge to the whole. If this simple test be applied, it will be found that here really lies the essential feature of the novel sensational.

Crime in fiction, however, was long unpopular, and, unless by the most vulgar writers, no attempt was made for many years to follow up Godwin's daring innovation; and probably the first serious endeavour to employ crime as a means for enforcing increased attention to a particular novel was made by Mrs. Catherine Crowe, who, in *Susan Hopley* and *Lily Dawson*, gave indications of the coming rich harvest to be reaped by more able workers from the combination of crime with mystery.

Two novels in particular, one by the late Wilkie Collins, the *Woman in White*, and *Lady Audley's Secret*, by Miss Braddon, are decidedly epochal books, each marking out a fresh sphere of action for novelists capable of inventing what may be called the puzzle plot. The *Woman in White* is, indeed, all in all, Wilkie Collins' most distinctive work. It was begun August, 1859, and finished in July in the following year. Issued first in *All the Year Round*, it appeared in three-volume shape August, 1860, and very soon after was translated into German and French. Time was indeed when, as suggested above, in what would be then called the respectable school of fiction, it was

virtually inadmissible to introduce to view the
whole machinery and detail of domestic life; but
the sensationalists soon perceived how rich and
practically inexhaustible a field could be opened
to the novelist who, with a Defoe-like verisimilitude, proved capable of working into some fatalistic
sequence of human experiences all the details of
contemporary life. In the stilted stories of our
grandmothers' days it would never have done to
enlist, as Wilkie Collins does, the aid of house-
maids, cooks, and policemen, in the work of developing the plot; while in Miss Braddon's long
series of novels, as, indeed, in all the salient
examples of this school of fiction, we have all the
conceivable circumstance of contemporary life in
every one of its phases placed at the disposition
of the novelist, and all are adroitly combined in his
service. Formerly, it was, for example, the custom
to omit the names of streets mentioned in a narrative, and to indicate towns, as D—— or N——,
while dates were rarely filled in. The sensational school of writers, commencing with the trium-
virate, Crowe, Collins, and Braddon, go more auda-
ciously to work; and all these details, which of old
imparted but vagueness to fiction, are now filled
in with the exactitude of newspaper reports; and
thus it has come about that fiction is made to
appear as fact. As a natural consequence, this

has led to the importation into current fiction of
the sensational type of very much, indeed, that
is fact; and in many cases the great effort of the
writer is simply how to suitably combine naturally
a set of incidents which are absolutely real! In
a word, it is only the plot and the characterisation
that form the original portions of many books of
this class.

In the sensational novel, pure and simple, all is
subordinated to the plot; and when once the end
is reached usually all further interest ceases. The
book is, in fact, to the reader like a display of
fireworks which fade ultimately into blackness;
but an increasing number of writers have perceived and seized on the obvious benefit of combining sensationalism with characterisation, and have
thus produced a far higher type of novel. In a
great degree this has been done by Charles Reade,
who, besides adopting sensationalism and characterisation, has given many of his novels a triple
strength by making them serve a purpose. Thus
in his splendid novel, *It is Never Too Late to Mend*,
we have a series of sensations, all resting on crime,
and yet redeemed by the genius of the writer from
ever sinking to the vulgar and the coarse.

It may be noted, indeed, that in nearly all of
Reade's exceedingly fine fictions, crime is the
pivot on which the action turns, as in the case of

8

the *Double Marriage*, *Hard Cash*, and many others.
But crime, treated as Reade treats it, is made to
yield its most salutary lessons ; and, as crime un-
happily exists, novels of this type may be justly
regarded as fulfilling an ethical as well as a
recreative purpose.   One of the most popular of
sensational novelists in his day was J. Sheridan
Le Fanu (who died 1874), the author of *Uncle
Silas*, *Wylder's Hand*, and other weird novels.   Le
Fanu had a method of his own, and was no copyist.
Few writers could paint better the peculiarities
and the mysteries of some of our old county
families, and he always rendered the still life
round his plots in a masterly way.   In the
Wyvern Mystery, he gives us quite a Rembrandt-
like portrait of Squire Fairfield of Wyvern.   Black,
dark, and drear is, he says, the winter of this stern
old man.   He does not acquiesce in the thought
of death for him.   Alice Maybell, the daughter
of the vicar whom he had cruelly wronged, is
taken to his hearth out of a secret remorse for his
conduct towards her dead father.   Alice herself is
a pretty, bright, simple girl, and illumines the
gloomy old hall with her charms and pretty ways.
The old man, discontented at his widowhood, and
believing that he has yet much life in him, con-
templates marrying this timid young girl, and
exalting her high in the county.   Lo and behold,

she is already married to one of his sons; and the
scenes that ensue when the old squire discovers
the truth are finely conceived. Harry and Charles,
the sons, are well delineated; and the story of the
horrible woman who is the one wife too many in
the book is fascinating. The scene in which this
infuriated woman tries to murder poor timid Alice
is terribly tragic.

Mrs. Henry Wood (1820-1887) has also employed crime in fiction, but it generally assumes
the milder forms of commercial fraud, etc.; and
regarded from the position here taken up, her
excellent and eminently entertaining novels are
hardly to be ranked under the heading of the
absolutely sensational. To what extremes, indeed, the rage for ultra-sensationalism may go is
shown in the *White Blind*, by F. A. Scudamore,
which begins with an attempt at wife murder,
leading to blackmailing by tramps, and includes
in its more startling incidents an endeavour to
destroy one of the female characters by placing her
before a steam roller in a public road and setting
it in motion while the engineer was away!

There is, in fact, a distinct tendency to do for the
sensational novel what has been done for the stage,
viz., to rely too greatly for effect on main force,
appeals to the senses and the coarser emotions,
and to enlist in the service of the writer all the

material agencies around us to intensify and colour
the narrative. At the same time, it must in justice
be said that in the case of many writers—Wilkie
Collins and Miss Braddon particularly—this tendency is found combined with the free exercise of
a painstaking art, and an earnest desire that
whatever heightens the effects of the tale shall
also point a moral.

Some of Mr. Walter Besant's many novels are
sensational, as *The World Went Very Well Then,*
wherein there are some strong elements; and in
collaboration with the late James Rice, Mr. Besant
produced some very interesting novels, strongly
inclining to the sensational. Mr. Joseph Hatton
(1839), in his *Cruel London, By Order of the Czar,*
and Miss Marryat (Mrs. Frances Lean), have written
in this vein; and so, too, have Mr. David Christie
Murray, James Payn, as in *By Proxy,* a good
example, and especially the late Robert Louis
Stevenson (noticed also under "Occult Novels")
in *Kidnapped,* with its murderous fight on ship-
board, the *Black Arrow,* and others, which are
all blood-curdling stories.

Mention should be made of Colonel P. Meadows
Taylor (1808-1876), who wrote a novel, *Confessions
of a Thug,* which is highly sensational, and yet based
on fact. On a far lower literary plane, but for a
while much more popular, was Mr. Frederick J.

Fargus (1847-1885), who, under the pen-name of "Hugh Conway," achieved, by his highly sensational story *Called Back*, a phenomenal if ephemeral success. Mr. Conan Doyle, the historical novelist already referred to, has also written several very sensational stories, of which the latest collection is entitled *Round the Red Lamp*. Harrison Ainsworth and others who have produced sensational novels are noticed under other sections. Julian Hawthorne, and some Australian sensational writers, will also be found duly dealt with under "American and Australian Novels".

CHAPTER X

OCCULT NOVELS AND NOVELS OF ADVENTURE.

WHY and how is it that of late in fiction the employment of things occult has come so much to the front ? Some of the greatest successes have of late years been achieved by works that our forefathers would certainly not have even tolerated.

It has been cynically remarked that where there is much mystery there is much evil. It would, however, be false to the facts to allege that the increasing popularity of the occult novel is due to any lurking belief that evil lies that way. There is, in truth, an intense and perfectly natural curiosity to penetrate behind the veil of which Tennyson speaks so mournfully in the *In Memoriam*. It is more even than—

> The desire of the moth for the star,
>   The night for the morrow,
> The yearning to something afar
>   From the sphere of our sorrow.

This passion, for such it is, for occultism resides in the deepest rooted instincts of the human soul; and in tracing out the genesis of the occult novel, properly so called, we find that even now, after so much has been done in this direction,—and need I add with the results of really leaving things truly supernatural just where they have always been?— we see still a succession of novels flowing on, dealing with hypnotic problems, esoteric Buddhism, theosophy and the like! I think I am right in identifying the first occult novel worthy of the name with *St. Leon*, William Godwin's work, brought out about a century ago, wherein the hero obtains an elixir of life; and among the many strange results is the confusion caused to the members of his family when he returns to them a young man, unknown, and about the age of his eldest daughter! Godwin, however, makes no attempt to explain aught of the mystery he creates. He works a kind of main force magic, and depends for his success on making his readers simply wonder. In *Zanoni*, Lord Lytton's development of *St. Leon*, consummate skill is employed in giving to the magic of the man who is virtually what used to be understood as a magician, the most advanced scientific and metaphysical culture, and the whole conception is rendered equally intellectual and interesting. In the *Strange Story*, Lord

Lytton made yet a further advance. He summoned to his aid other resources of science, and blending in the crucible of a passionate love-story the most elaborate metaphysics and biological discoveries of his day, produced thence some effects which yet remain very fine, and ·stamp him as in all things the master of this form of art. Finally, in the *Coming Race* we have a new and an entirely original development of this occult phase of the novel, and even the creation of a new type of thinking creatures, which, perhaps, most of all, nobly crowns his fame as a creative novelist.

One of the most dreadful of occult novels is, I should say, *Frankenstein*, written by Mary Wollstonecraft Godwin (1759-1797), the second wife of Shelley, the poet, and the daughter of the author of *St. Leon.* In *Frankenstein* a student of biology conceives the appalling idea of making a man in his laboratory; and, as may be imagined by those who have not read this terrible fiction, the novel reads like a frightful nightmare. It is, indeed, a book whereon I do not like to dwell; and, to my thinking, it entirely transcends the proper province of fiction; but of its weird, and at times fearful power over any reader who once takes it up, there can be no doubt. Mrs. Shelley wrote some other novels. Among the number are: *Valperga, the Last Man, Lodore,* and the *Fortunes of Perkin War-*

beck. In *Frankenstein* horror is especially wrought up to a terrible pitch, owing to the fact, as set forth in the appalling narrative, that the monster man, supposed to be chemically and physiologically made in a secret laboratory, commits a murder, and the wretched author of the creature perceives too late what he has done in fashioning such a monster, whose mission is destruction, and who is quite devoid of all moral qualities. Possibly, read in a right spirit, there is much highly suggestive and advanced moral teaching to be gained from this narrative, which, nevertheless, must be to some persons far too harrowing to read with any real satisfaction. On a lower plane by far of creation must be placed some of the works of Mrs. Crowe, who, in 1848, produced the *Night Side of Nature*, a history of the supernatural, and a series of fictions followed, under the title of *Light and Darkness, or Mysteries of Life*.

It has been said that faith in the supernatural fails in proportion as people are more instructed in physics; but where has this faith wholly disappeared? If even science demonstrated the impossibility of a disembodied spirit becoming visible to the living, the faith that after all it might do so would remain in many; and would not that faith be a phenomenon in itself possessing deep and awful interest? Doubtless some recorded instances of

so-called apparitions are due directly to cerebral
disorders, but does that touch the real question at
issue? In 1791 Mr. Nicolai, a Berlin bookseller,
was haunted by phantasms believed to be purely
the coinage of his own brain; and his notes thereon
are to be found in the *Transactions of the Berlin
Philosophical Society*. To deduce thence that *all*
such phenomena must be due to cerebral disease
would be manifestly absurd. In 1662 the daughter
of Sir Charles Lee saw the apparition of her de-
ceased brother, who warned her of death at noon the
following day; and this happened, although the
young lady was quite well, so far as could be seen.
Dr. Donne, the famous divine, was the subject of a
somewhat similar warning; and there are, without
going to Mr. Stead's *Borderland*, very many well-
accredited and perfectly unaccountable apparitions
in all lands and among all peoples. There is ob-.
viously an unseen world; and to dogmatise as some
do as to what can and cannot be, is certainly
highly unphilosophical. Many sceptics affect indifference to aught that is not, as they say, matter of
fact; and surely we may retort, with a better intent
than that of the sneering Pilate, and ask, "What *is*
matter of fact?" Let us take one view of the matter
which naturally suggests itself. During only one
century some thousand millions of human beings
are born, and all are undoubtedly different the one

from the other and each from the rest. In music we have had as yet but one Handel, and in poetry but one Shakespeare. Now, what I want to draw particular attention to is this—if it happens, as we know it does, that now and then a human being is born endowed with intellectual powers exceeding those of all others, why may not some be born possessing perceptive faculties for seeing phenomena that are completely hidden from others? Science may here be well invoked to testify against its own scepticism. We are assured that no particles composing any substance in our physical world are in absolute contact. Even in so hard and dense a body as a diamond, interstices are universal. Might not a person then be born able to perceive these? Of course, science replies no such being has appeared; but this is not an answer to the question, and it is perfectly conceivable that in some among us there are latent perceptive faculties, as there are latent powers of impressing and influencing others, which probably in the majority of instances go down to the grave unknown because unused, and unused only because occasion never came to put them to any practical test. This is decidedly a common-sense view to take of the supernatural; and it suggests very clearly, I think, some of the reasons why the whole subject is beset with such peculiar difficulty directly one attempts to investigate it.

Another and deeper question arises in regard to what is known as the occult. Is it principally a matter of greater knowledge? This is the view that many writers have taken of the whole thing. One says: "Magic! what is magic? When the traveller in Persia beholds the ruins of palaces and temples, the ignorant inhabitants inform him that they were the work of magicians! What is beyond their own power, the vulgar cannot comprehend to be lawfully in the power of others. But if by magic you mean a perpetual research amongst all that is more latent and obscure in Nature, I answer, I profess that magic, and that he who does so comes but nearer to the fountain of all belief." In a remarkable work, entitled *Demonology and Witchcraft*, by Robert Brown, we are plainly told that the Old Testament first and the New Testament afterwards, teach that there is a kind of sorcery, and that it arises out of the conflict between good and evil, and is due to the permitted operations, within certain limits of time and space, of the prince of the powers of the air, in other words, of Satan. The history of familiar spirits, or demons, is traced out until we come to the Gospels, wherein they certainly appear very prominently; and wherein, too, as a perpetual rebuke to the rationalists of our own day, they all evidently know quite well that Christ is the Son of

God, and so tremble at His Presence. The same writer reminds us that idolatry and witchcraft were first openly practised in the plain of Shinar, in the Babylon of old; and this spirit of unspeakable depravity is traced out in the rites of all savage tribes; and it is further shown that the Egyptian magicians of the days of Moses were sorcerers whose successors still remain in some pagan parts of the world unto this day.

A curious article appeared over forty years ago in the *Quarterly Review*, wherein an account is given of wonders performed by a band of Bengal jugglers before an Indian potentate. One of their most astonishing feats was the power of fixing objects in the air, seemingly without any support. Thus, one juggler, operating out of doors, took a bow and shot an arrow upward, which appeared at a certain height to be fixed. He then aimed thereat a second arrow, which attached itself to the first, and so on, until the last of all striking that nearest to the earth of those suspended, the whole broke up, and fell, when they appeared to be changed to a chain of some seventy-five feet long. The juggler tossed one end up, and it seemed to hook on to some invisible support. A dog was then brought forward, and immediately ran up the chain and disappeared; and in succession other creatures were, to all appearance, thus disposed of. In the end, the juggler took down the chain and put it in a bag; and the narrator and no one had the smallest notion of the way in which the animals had thus been got rid of. In Persia and Hindostan, Mr. Brown further reminds us, some sects practise the art of simulating death as part of their ritual. Sir Claude M. Wade, agent to the British Government at the Court of Runjeet Singh, witnessed the seeming resuscitation of a fakir who had been buried forty days. All this, Mr. Brown remarks, simply bears out the well-known statement of Holy Scripture, that there shall arise false Christs (Buddha was, I suppose, one), and false prophets, and shall show great signs and wonders, insomuch that, if it were possible, they shall deceive the very elect. Every one has heard of the familiar trick of Indian jugglers in growing a mango out of doors, seemingly anywhere on the hard trodden road, and of the famous basket trick, and of similar tricks, which remain so far insoluble problems to the curious. The performance of marvellous feats of simulated magic on prepared stages under cover as in our own country, and aided by the best resources of mechanical and chemical science, is quite a different thing from what is accomplished by some Oriental jugglers; Mr. Brown's general position seems borne out by much historic evidence. Mr. Grant Allen has himself woven a terrible tale based on the abominable snake worship of some of the West Indian blacks; and the idea appears to be reasonable, as put forth by some who have investigated modern sorcery, that it may be a new form of that very ancient devil worship of which examples still survive among some of the most benighted savages. William Godwin, it is worthy of note, wrote a work called the *Lives of the Necromancers;* but in his *St. Leon* he is careful, as I have already said, to avoid touching on aught of the arcana of the black arts, and gives no hint of the sources whence his hero, St. Leon, drew the elixir of life, which to him proved, after all, little better than a curse. *St. Leon* is the forerunner of the elixir of life idea in English fiction. The first Lord Lytton doubtless had it in view when he constructed *Zanoni;* and in that extraordinary story we are carried, as it were, out of the very edge of the line that divides us from the supernatural. In *Frankenstein,* a fiction of an unhallowed art, we are introduced to perhaps a hint, a glimpse, of what may be conveniently called the forbidden side of man's misapplied effort to penetrate the mysteries of life and death. Withal, one cannot well resist the conclusions of those who would trace all tampering of this kind to the biblical account of the falling away of many of the ancient Jews--

people and priests—into idolatry. It is distinctly
stated in the Bible that Manasseh did that which
was evil in the sight of Jehovah, like unto the
abominations of the heathen. Then we are told
further that enchantments were used; and finally
it is solemnly declared that Manasseh made Judah
to do worse than the heathen. Now, in direct reference to this, David says, they did not destroy the
nations concerning whom God commanded them.
No doubt, in these latter days, and especially
among Western peoples, living in a materialised
and generally personally comfortable civilisation,
the true significance of all this is nearly if not
quite missed.   Many fierce attacks have been
made on the Scriptures because of what appears
to us the severity of the injunctions laid on the
Jews to destroy the heathen whom they dispos-
sessed of the promised land. But we see these
things from the side only of humanity and mercy;
we truly know not what was the enormity of
wickedness that existed among the races given up
to idolatry; and, perhaps, it is unfortunate, for a
right understanding of what it all means, that we
do not usually perceive that idolatry is really a
serving of the devil. That worship survives in
changed forms: but who can say what had been
the blessed results if the ancient people of God
had rigidly obeyed the commands laid upon them,

and spared nothing that was in direct antagonism to the God who singled them out from all the races of men, to preserve His pure worship, and prepare the way for Christianity? In this matter the New Testament abundantly confirms the Old. In Matthew, for example, the Saviour very plainly declares regarding possession by demons, that Satan (the Satan who tempted Him) is their Prince, and that they help for a time to sustain what is the Kingdom of Evil.

The sum and substance of all is that a black art has existed from the fall of man, and that in each era it appears in forms and fashion suited to the age and the prevailing modes of thought and feeling. Hence we may take it, that such matters as hypnotism—when genuine, and not a mere parody — such manifestations as certain theosophists make, and the like, are all radically akin to the idolatry denounced in the Bible, and should be avoided as an utter abomination. Such things are surely dishonour to God, and if blindly persisted in, may lead to that alienation from light and truth whose final end is but confusion and despair.

Before passing on to later times I should add that Mrs. Catherine Crowe (*née* Miss Stevens), who was born in 1800, began her literary career by publishing a tragedy. Thence she passed to

9

prose fiction, and wrote *Manorial Rights*, a novel, followed by the *Adventures of Susan Hopley*, which, as a story of incident, met with much favour, and was dramatised.

The great contemporary exponent of the occult in fiction, so far as one work goes, was the late Robert Louis Stevenson, whose masterpiece in many respects is *Dr. Jekyll and Mr. Hyde*, quite as original a work as *Frankenstein*. This relates to the double personality of a man who included in himself a latent monster! Here, too, there is undoubtedly a fine and most wholesome moral, only it is not in the least obtruded, and must be found out by the reader for himself. The art wherewith the animalism that lies latent in this character is roused to life is consummate; and we have here the suggestion, so finely given in the *Strange Story* of the first Lord Lytton, that animalism alone, *plus* intellect only, is diabolical.

Evidently, there is a growing disposition on the part of readers for books of magic, wherein the imagination of the writer can revel at will in all things conceivable and many inconceivable. The reason for producing such books on the writer's part is not far to seek. There can be no doubt that the avenues of what may be called the legitimate fiction of the past, are being in a measure blocked by the more marked successes

of those who have filled them with real masterpieces. To take an example : since the first Lord
Lytton's *Harold*, there has been and is little
encouragement to any historical novelist to com-
pose a romance dealing with the Norman Conquest
of England ; although, by the way, Sir Charles
James Napier, the conqueror of Scinde, did com-
pose a fine novel on Harold ; but, naturally enough,
it has been completely overshadowed by Lord
Lytton's splendid romance on the same subject.
It is probable that a consciousness of this has had
much influence in stimulating departures from
what may be conveniently called the beaten
tracks of imaginative literature. Fancy has been
invoked to aid imagination ; and thus it has come
about that a late phase of the novel has been to
impart to it much of the character of an Arabian
Nights' story. In a word, we have to deal with a
revulsion from the mere occult novel, like *Zanoni*,
A Strange Story, and a simple flight into those
realms of pure fancy, where the writer is, indeed,
an absolute sovereign, reigning supreme on the
one condition that he amuses.

Mr. Anstey's *Vice Versâ* is a novel belonging to
this type. In it we have as the central pivotal
idea the obviously whimsical notion of a father,
a selfish, pompous man of business, changing
places with his little boy and going to school,

while the son stays at home in the outward seeming of the father! This opens the way obviously
to an infinite variety of humorous and funny con-
ceits, and to not a little fun of the excruciating
kind. Here the modern magic is worked through
the medium of a mysterious stone,—of course,
from that home of all that is occult, the Orient.
This book achieved a phenomenal success, and
distinctly opened up new avenues of fiction.

Mr. Anstey is indeed supreme monarch in the
enchanted realm of phantasy, resting, however, on
a basis of every-day life circumstances. In his
later work, the *Pariah,* the scene opens at Trouville,
and is very interesting. Allen Chadwick, an illite-
rate and vulgar young man, is the pariah ; and the
book is full of those amusing incidents which render
Mr. Anstey such an entertaining fictionist.

This species of Arabian Nights' magic has now
infected other novelists. Mr. Walter Besant has
even taken a hint from Mr. Anstey by writing a
novel called the *Doubts of Dives,* wherein we
have two friends, both cultured and intellectual,
the one rich and idle, the other poor and obliged
to work. The rich man is a grumbler; and after
mutual confessions, each thinks how much he
would like to be the other! Eh, presto! The
rich one remembers a certain rare liquid distilled
in a wondrous way, enclosed in a small box, and

procured mysteriously at Damascus. This potent
liquor has the effect, if taken under certain mes-
meric conditions, of enabling two persons to exchange identities! This the two friends do for
three months,—a time-limit being, it seems, compatible with the use of this strange essence ; and, the
exchange being effected, each is at first delighted,
the one with the prospect of having to work for
his living, and the other with that of living entirely
at his ease for some time to come. Mr. Besant,
as may be supposed, works out the humours of the
unique situation with much skill ; and the narrative holds the reader with a firm grip until the
very end. Obviously, entire originality, combined
with, at least, reasonable verisimilitude, is the
key to the charm of books like *Vice Versâ*. In
Francis and Frances, by H. Edwards, we have decidedly an extraordinary conception. Here the
story is opened through the agency of a Dr. Ditch-
burn, who attends Mrs. Jutland, the mother of
twins as like as two peas. The unhappy father
expires in a fit at something, no one exactly knows
what, that has happened to the twins; and soon
we learn that periodically one of the twins dis-
appears. The twins are christened Francis and
Frances, and the neighbours wonder, as well they
may, why the children are christened *separately*.
As the twins grow up, very amazing things result.

Thus, we are told, it was very well to teach Francis the days of the week in their proper order, but not so well to get him to understand that, though he was then saying his lessons on a Thursday, the next day for *him* was Saturday. In like manner is it with Frances. In a word, this very whimsical novel is a sort of dissolving view of twins, only one of whom appears at a time; and, as may be imagined, this singular abnormal mode of alternate existence is made to give rise to a series of really absurd as well as extraordinary situations.

" Rita," a well-known novelist, has produced a work of the occult sort under the title of the *Seventh Dream*, wherein we have the old idea worked out, that a dream-power may be cultivated like any other faculty at will; and the hero of the story, Alured Marvel, falls into a trance and sees therein a lovely woman; and the old man who casts him into this charming trance promises to give him these dreams *ad libitum* if he will consent to transfer his will to him, the old wizard, for seven days. The compact is struck, and Alured is introduced in a trance to Nyleta, the white queen who lives in a wondrous city. Eventually the reader is not greatly surprised to find that there has been a murder committed by Alured during his dreams, his form having been borrowed

for that purpose by the old man who confers on him
the faculty of dreaming beautiful dreams. The
story is unique for " Rita "; but the dream-idea
may be found in one of the beautiful tales composing that charming phantasy of the first Lord
Lytton's, the *Pilgrims of the Rhine*. One more
mysterious work of this kind is that entitled *A
Strange Manuscript found in a Copper Cylinder*. Here
the narrative opens on board a yacht becalmed
off Madeira. A copper cylinder is fished up, and
found to contain a papyrus manuscript. The
yachtsmen beguile the tedium of the calm by de-
ciphering what proves to be a tale of the wildest
invention. The hero is one Adam More, who,
with one companion, gets lost in the Antarctic
regions. The "natives," of what are believed to
be uninhabited regions, are described as small,
thin, shrivelled and black, with hideous faces.
They are likened to animated mummies, and include women described as horrible " hags ". More
escapes, losing his companion, in a boat, and somehow (the " how " is easy to the magic of fiction)
passes into quite a new world of an extraordinary
character, both physically and morally. The light
of the strange region described is stated to be a
perfect blaze of moteless splendour, and both the
flora and fauna are new, although both are referable to what geology has revealed as the physical

world before the flood.   More falls in with a strange
maiden known as Almah, and among other marvels
rides on a kind of mighty winged horse, called the
Athaleb.   Indeed, the writer has had the ingenuity
to invent a kind of language, as well as quite a
new world of altogether strange beings.   Marvels
thicken; for in this singular land it is found that
the poor are held in the greatest esteem; and
everybody strives earnestly to be poor—a thing
extremely difficult to be, as every one is heaping
gifts on every one else; and then in races and other
competitions the great aim is to *lose;* and thence, as
may be readily supposed, very curious and extremely
amusing complications result.   Another striking
story of the marvellous is the *Secret of the Llamas*.
Here the hero, an officer sent to carry on a survey in
Northern India, falls down a precipice, and being
picked up by some member of a caravan, is carried
to Thibet, and there sold into slavery, becoming a
servant of the Grand Llama, who takes an interest
in him, and eventually initiates him into many
mysteries of the temple where he officiates. The hero
all along nurses the hope of escape, but is compelled
to dissemble and appear willing to conform to the
worship of the place. Some exceedingly marvellous
"manifestations" take place; and eventually the
hero does escape, and arriving safely in England
finds his lady-love has married an unprincipled

gambler on the Stock Exchange, who is slowly poisoning her to secure her property to himself. Then begins an intensely interesting description of the way in which the hero of the book employs his esoteric knowledge to frustrate all this wickedness. A decided merit of the book is the straightforward and thoroughly realistic manner of the narration.

Some of the marked successes of our own day are referable, however, to works that have long fallen into an undeserved neglect.

Every great work of fiction does not exactly succeed even when published, in precise proportion to its merits. The *Life and Adventures of Peter Wilkins* is, to some extent, a case in point. The sub-title states that the work is by a Cornish man, and relates particularly to his shipwreck near the South Pole, his wonderful passage through a subterraneous cavern into a kind of new world; his there meeting with a gawrey, or flying woman, whose life he preserved, and afterwards married her ; and, finally, his extraordinary conveyance to the country of glumms and gawreys, or men and women that fly. Now we have here, in a sense, the germ of the first Lord Lytton's fine romance of the *Coming Race*, wherein the winged people are wrought up in so effective a manner. It is curious, however, that beyond his name, or what

is believed to be his name—Robert Pultock—
nothing is known of the author. Yet, it seems
highly probable that the singular and purely imaginary beings mentioned in *Peter Wilkins*, the
glumms and gawreys, furnished Southey with his
notion of the Glendowers in his fine but neglected
poem, the *Curse of Kehama*. One of the features
in *Peter Wilkins* is the glossary of words invented
by the writer, which undoubtedly displays great
ingenuity: thus *ors clam gee* means "here am I".
Altogether this effort of mingled fancy and imagination possesses very great merit. The first
edition of this work appeared in 1750, was in two
duodecimo volumes, and was inscribed to Elizabeth,
Countess of Northumberland. It was not for
eighty-five years that the name of the author
was accidentally found to be Robert Pultock, or,
perhaps, Poltock; and all that is known about him
is, that one of that name lies buried at Lyme
Church, Dorsetshire. Was it the one production
of the writer's literary genius? The book did not
make any stir on its appearance, although now an
early copy is worth £8 or £9. From *Peter Wilkins*
have been drawn ideas for pantomimes, and while
Coleridge admired it greatly, Southey declared
that Pultock's winged people constituted "the
most beautiful creatures of imagination that ever
were devised".

It is curious that just as prose fiction rose out of romance largely mingled with sentiment and poetry, so in the later nineteenth-century days the novel has evinced decided tendencies to break away from all bounds and run into romance. The "sensational" novel doubtless prepared the way for this; and it may be in part due to the fact that, for a long while, the literature for the young has been very largely furnished by such ultra-romancists as Jules Verne, Gustav Aimard, Mayne Reid, Kingston, and very many others; the result is, that boys thus fed on romance are apt to incline that way in their tastes when they grow up. Properly speaking, novelists simply seize on incidents of the day, and endeavour to portray such men and women as we are all more or less familiar with. The novelist, indeed, does not supply very much invention of his own; his business is to harmonise, to proportion, to co-ordinate plot and *motif*, and to impart symmetry to a mass of sayings and doings, and above all to render them interesting. From this point of view, indeed, the conventional novelist may be rightly regarded as an editor of miscellaneous material, drawn from all sources and concerning people, places and things : and to these he has to impart the grace and unity of a fine work of art. His skill appears in the manner wherein he manipulates and manages his materials, and withal he is obliged to move within certain well-defined limits.   Now, as has been aptly said, the weaver of romance can and does go where he lists, and do almost whatever he pleases with his plot, his incidents, and his characters.   He may literally soar into the skies, as a popular serial writer has lately done, and give us an account of impossible aerial ships seemingly suggested by Tennyson's terrible vision when he—

Heard the heavens fill with shouting, and there rained a
    ghastly dew
From the nations' airy navies grappling in the central blue.

Or the weaver of romance may dive into the depths of the earth, as in the *Coming Race;* and here we find a marked return to the invention and methods of the author of *Peter Wilkins,* of *Gulliver,* of Horace Walpole and the *Castle of Otranto,* of Mrs. Shelley's *Frankenstein,* of *Zanoni,* and the like.

Mrs. Behn in her *Oronooko* gave us very long ago a foreshadowing of such romance as is in *The World Went Very Well Then;* and the principle was carried on in the *Romance of the Forest* and in the *Monk* of Matthew Lewis.   One immediate effect undoubtedly of the outburst of romantic fiction late in the nineteenth century has been to greatly enlarge the domains of the novel and to relax the canons of its art.   There is, in fact, a sort of fusion at work between the two great types and the distinctive forms of prose fiction : the romance is imparting variety and colour to the novel, and in its turn the novel is imparting to romance realism. Will the two forms ultimately be inextricably blended ? Finally among books of adventure which have attained to very great popularity, although not exactly " occult," mention may be made of those by " Q " (Mr. Quiller Couch) which attained to great popularity in a very short time : *I Saw Three Ships* is the quaint title of one, while the latest is the *Delectable Duchy*, in which the Cornish peasant and fisherman have been made the text of some twenty stories or sketches wherein there is much pathos.

I have now cited enough to indicate what a wealth of variety and what intensity of interest may be found in this class of fiction.

CHAPTER XI

POPULAR NOVELS OF THE PAST, WITH
REMARKS ON SOME OF THE PRESENT.

THE present choice of novels, even those of a single class, is now so wide and varied, that we can hardly realise how it was with our forefathers, especially in remote country houses, when, perhaps, a dozen different works of fiction were all that the novel reader could draw on at a time.

Once, strange as it may now seem, even Samuel Richardson was a fashionable novelist, and as an exponent of women stood decidedly foremost. Let it be borne in mind that, with but a few exceptions, all Richardson's correspondents and friends were women; he was twice married, and it was not until he had attained the age of fifty, that he took up the *rôle* of novelist: more than this, he had constant companionship among young women, and he was always ready in asking, and, what is more, in taking advice as to "points" in his novels, and hence he may be said to have truly reflected in his books, as in a faithful mirror, the manners and tone of the female world of his day. He was not confined either to the world of London, in which he himself lived : Lady Bradshaigh, one of his literary correspondents, lived in Lancashire, and Madame Klopstock wrote to him from the Fatherland. Surely this is the true reason why Richardson's novels have a certain feminine atmosphere about them, and why his women are far more interesting than his men. This was undoubtedly the reason too, why Rousseau—himself a champion of the sex—waxed so eloquent over Clarissa, and why Alfred de Musset declared it " le premier roman du monde ".

In those days, from a scarcity of books, reading for recreation was exceedingly deliberate for the most part, compared with the present mode of galloping through a volume or two in a single day.

A correspondent of the *Gentleman's Magazine*, writing in 1852, has some pertinent remarks on " Country Book Clubs Fifty Years Ago," and after pointing out that in those days there were many good solid books to read, such as the works of Burke, Gibbon, Hume, Robertson, Dr. Johnson, and a long series of " Annual Registers " and the like, added : " Works of fiction were not numerous. We had neither Fielding, nor Richardson, nor, I think, Smollett. . . . We began with Madame d'Arblay, Madame de Genlis, and Dr. Moore,

whose *Zelucco* and *Edward* were well read.   Then
came the whole series of Mrs. Opie's novels and
tales. . . . Godwin also, with his political specula-
tions and his powerful novels; Miss Edgeworth,
in due time, with her exquisite fictions; Miss
Hamilton, Hannah More and Miss Hawkins."

And yet at a much earlier period to this it is
clear (so little is there that is really new under the
sun) that "society" greatly resembled what we
find it to be now in its more volatile and frivolous
phases.   The poet Young, in a satire on the women
of his day, says:—

> Britannia's daughters, much more fair than nice,
> Too fond of admiration, lose their price;
> Worn in the public eye, give cheap delight
> To throngs and tarnish to the sated sight,
> As unreserved and beauteous as the sun,
> Thro' every sign of vanity they run;
> Assemblies, parks, coarse feasts in city halls,
> Lectures and trials, plays, committees, balls,
> Wells, bedlams, executions, Smithfield scenes,
> And fortune tellers' caves and lions' dens,
> Taverns, exchanges, bridewells, drawing rooms,
> Instalments, pillories, coronations, tombs,
> Tumblers, and funerals, puppet shows, reviews,
> Sales, races, rabbits, and, still stranger, pews.

How modern all this is!

Novel reading!   The two words form a mighty
talisman far beyond aught we read of in Arabian
story.   What is Aladdin's lamp in comparison?

for in this spell of power we have past, present, and future at our intellectual command. It is a spell that places us within mental hearing and sympathetic touch of the best society of the world; and, if our curiosity runs that way, of the world at large—we can summon up, by the magic of page-turning, the wise, the witty, the brave, the beautiful, the good, the gentle, and the pure ; and thus the reader is veritably made a citizen of the world, and that in the most complete way possible.

All antiquity is at the command of the reader of fiction. For him or her the gates of the Past roll back at the opening of the book; and, lo! what a wealth of enjoyment! What a rapture of variety lies at the command of the reader! He can converse with kings and emperors, with the heroes and conquerors of the earth; he can travel whither he will, and see such marvels as pass his imagination to conceive; he can revel in the most splendid scenery; participate in the wildest adventures, and sympathetically aid in the greatest and noblest of deeds. Or he may retire into the most complete rural simplicity, and dream away his soul in sylvan peace; or he may struggle and starve and triumph in the competitive press of city life; or, if frivolously disposed, cannot he participate in the humours of life, live mentally among the witty, and laugh out his soul, like Rabelais, shaking in

his easy chair? Nay, more, far more, he may
incline to the novel with a purpose, and learn
thence in the most delightful of ways practical
politics, philosophy, and philanthropy, or study
theology, or learn something of everything that
occupies the thoughts of men.   He may incline to
novels of the navy or the army, of sport or fashion;
and thus in fancy, with an effortless pleasure, the
reader is for the time, to all intellectual intents
and purposes, a sailor, soldier, sportsman or gentleman at large. Is this phantasy only? Surely
not.   Call it illusion, dreaming, what you will;
but confess that while the spell of fiction is in
force on the engrossed and all-absorbed reader,
the pleasure derived thence and the impressions
received are, for the time, true and real enough.
Indeed, what enjoyment within human reach of a
purely individual and personal character and concentrated on one alone, can come near the pure
and rapturous all-absorbing abandonment to the
overmastering spell of fiction? Here, indeed, the
poorest, the weakest, the most timid as to enterprise or exertions of his own, may feel himself
truly the heir of all the ages; and observe that it is
through this spell that we can enjoy communion
with the most gifted minds and the most sympathetic and expansive souls of the world's best of
humanity in all times.   To some of us intercourse

of this kind in the flesh is indeed restricted, and
to many it is prohibited; but the book once opened
sets that straight, and restores the balance that
has been lost between the rich and the poor.   We
have through novels, intercourse with the best of
all minds; and thus the solitary reader is insensibly
refined and exalted by familiar intercourse with
that spirit of fiction so called—for fiction is truth
after all, in its really good form,—which is one of
the most civilising agencies of the times.

That there is good, great and enduring, far-
reaching and widely influential, in novel reading,
as well as pleasure, keen and intense, ever varying
and ever fresh, needs hardly any special demonstra-
tion.   It has been well said that a bad novel is one
without a soul; and certainly to deal only with
superficial life, and leave unsounded the depths of
feelings and passion, is to spoil any novel as to its
interest, and to ensure that it will soon be cast
aside as being altogether unsatisfactory.   On the
other hand, it is clear that such fiction as really
embraces with a broad but sympathetic touch all
types of mankind, and more or less unravels their
life-threads, cannot fail to widen and deepen the
lives, too, of readers; and in disclosing thus the
destinies of many of whom we should otherwise
remain quite ignorant, what separating walls are
thrown down, and how much prejudice and

narrowness of thought and feeling are dissipated
for evermore! The really good and worthy
novelist necessarily brings us into the closest contact with fine and noble natures, with gentle and
loving hearts, with lofty aspirations, and with,
in a word, the *best* side of human nature. At the
same time, we have warning examples drawn from
the worse sides of life; while in great novels of this
comprehensive type, we have, as a consequence,
all the refining, purifying effect which the ancient
Greeks derived from the study of their matchless
tragedies—plays enacted by daylight, in the fresh
free air, and devoid of all the feverish and utterly
demoralising elements which too often belong to
the contemporary stage.

In a brief little known essay, De Quincey, dealing
with novels, remarks that a false ridicule has settled
thereon, and on young ladies as the readers thereof. He points out that, after all, the great commanding event, the one sole revolution in a
woman's life, is marriage; and thence the novel
is obviously to her the most interesting of books.
With men there are two master passions—ambition
and avarice; but, as De Quincey observes further,
a perfect miser is a great and therefore an extremely rare man, for very unusual qualities are
required to constitute the miser; and, if we fully
analyse the thing, we shall find that the roots of

ambition are generally struck deep in the soil of home, and fed with the sweet waters of affection. All the ambition of Clive, that greatest, perhaps, of our Indian warrior statesmen, was, after all, concentrated on the rehabilitation of his ancestral home; and, probed deeply enough, the motive power of most novels will be found identical with the ultimate forces that in its men of mark move the world.

But to return to Samuel Richardson: we have in *Pamela, or Virtue Rewarded,* a study of a female who has undoubtedly exercised a highly suggestive influence over many subsequent fiction-writers. Pamela, the heroine, is an artless girl of fifteen at the outset, who is exposed to the wicked wiles of a young aristocrat, who lays siege to her virtue in various ways; but is at length quite subdued by her thorough goodness, and is finally driven, by esteem as well as by love, to make her his wife.

Clarissa Harlowe, however, is considered by most, perhaps, as Richardson's masterpiece. Here again the heroine is a pure-minded and amiable girl, who is coerced by an ambitious parent to marry a man every way unworthy of her. She revolts at this, and even promises never to marry at all, sooner than to take for a husband a man whom she can neither esteem nor love. Another trial awaits her, and her troubles undoubtedly interest and lure the reader on.

In regard to Henry Fielding, it is certain that his characters are drawn with a powerful realism, before the word had come into use; and as an observer of human nature he is perhaps superior to Richardson, but his work is disfigured by an inherent coarseness which was peculiar to his times, and which Richardson certainly avoided.

Passing on to a later period, there was, during a considerable part of the present century, a long series of novels which were usually designated as "fashionable," and not without reason. They seem to have been written, for a great part, on the assumption that "the base and mechanical portion of the community," as the high-flown language of the times would have expressed it, were not only no readers of light literature, but that their ways, doings, and thoughts, could not by any possibility interest or concern the ladies and gentlemen of the period; hence there came a series of novels in which the action was carried on with unceasing decorum, by exquisitely dressed and well-mannered ladies and gentlemen, entirely artificial and generally quite unnatural. Some examples of this school are, however, by no means devoid of merit; and Robert Plumer Ward, a statesman of the times, wrote three novels, *De Vere, Tremaine, or the Man of Refinement*, and *De Clifford*, which are worth reading, as they illustrate well the tone of the early part of the nineteenth century.

The fashionable novel proper came, however, after a while, to be almost stereotyped as to certain of its features. The stock incidents included duels and elopements, and the third volume always ended with a wedding. There was of necessity a hero, who was *de rigueur* handsome and morally perfect, and a heroine who was beautiful and good ; in most cases a villain was added, who invariably came to a bad end. One of the first to elevate this type of writing to almost the highest level whereto it could attain, was Mrs. Catharine Grace Gore, the daughter of an English wine merchant, who, marrying an officer in the army, found herself eventually compelled to support her family by her pen. Mrs. Gore's initial novel was *Theresa Marchmont, or the Maid of Honour ;* and in such works as *Cecil, A Peer,* the *Banker's Wife,* etc., she probably indicated the way to a later school of fictionists, who saw how the fashionable could be developed into the domestic novel. Mrs. Anne Marsh, the author of *Two Old Men's Tales, Emilia Wyndham, Father Darcy, Time the Avenger,* and other works, may be bracketed with Mrs. Gore ; while in Mrs. Frances Trollope, the gifted mother of the two novelists, Anthony and Thomas Adolphus, we recognise a writer of power and

versatility, who once commanded a large reading
public. The *Widow Barnaby* is especially good.
Then we had Miss Jewsbury, whose fine novel *Zoe*
is full of passion and of nicely graduated character
sketches, and probably startled some of those who
desired the fashionable novel to remain unnatural.

Ostensibly the famous Theodore Hook was a
fashionable novelist, who sought at first no doubt
to supply the demand of the day; but in his *Jack
Brag*, wherein a young tallow-chandler apes the
gentleman, and in his fine character piece of *Gilbert
Gurney*, he rather broke through bounds, and fore-
shadowed the wider field to be embraced, when
the novel should be quite emancipated from almost
every kind of rule, canon, or restraint; so that there
is nothing new under the sun, or within the com-
pass of the wit of man to devise, that cannot and
may not be "worked up" for our delight in the
form of fiction. Miss Letitia Elizabeth Landon
("L. E. L.") (better known in connection with her
poetry) wrote several three-volume fashionable
novels, one being called *Romance and Reality*. A
word must be given to Mrs. Anna Eliza Bray, who
came of an old Cornish family, and on being married
to a son of Stothard the painter, visited the continent.
In Flanders her husband was killed while sketching
an old church; and eventually the widow, who went
to live in Devonshire, was married to the Rev.

Edward K. Bray. Then she began a series of romances, *De Foix*, and the *White Hoods*, dealing with the mediæval troubles between the nobles and citizens in Flanders, and *Talba, or the Moor of Portugal*. One of the most prolific novelists of the early part of the nineteenth century was William Harrison Ainsworth, who was by birth a member of a very ancient Lancashire family, and was born in 1805. He was educated at a Manchester grammar school, articled to a solicitor at sixteen; and ere he was of age, such was the precocity of his literary talent, he had published the romance of *Sir John Chiverton*. His early marriage with the daughter of a publisher induced him to abandon law for literature; and in 1834 his *Rookwood* took the public fancy, and made him famous. *Jack Sheppard* appeared serially, and increased his popularity; but its immorality has been justly held up to scathing criticism; and in the long series of successful novels and romances that flowed for years from Mr. Ainsworth's pen, there was an abundance of the " properties " of the historic past, but little of what is properly known as literature. Notwithstanding this, some of these fictions contain the results of a good deal of painstaking research into the past; and doubtless many young readers have received no little instruction from their pages.

Another most prolific novelist on a much higher plane is Anthony Trollope, who, divesting the original typical fashionable novel of all that was inherently false, artificial and ridiculous, to present-day notions, gave us, in such novels as *Orley Farm*, the *Small House at Allington* (containing Lily Dale, the best of all his female characters), in *Can You Forgive Her?* and a host of others, very exact transcripts from middle-class life, with a little of the upper ten thrown in now and then to heighten the effect.

En passant, in *Framley Parsonage*, to my thinking, Trollope sounds a deeper note of domestic life, and teaches a sterner and more useful lesson, than is his wont. Mark the fortune-favoured vicar, blessed with a lucrative living and a devoted wife. He has all the virtues indeed, but they are nearly neutralised by his weakness for exalted society, and his inability to say "no" to a hearty, jovial, frank, but false friend. He puts his name to paper, and soon is in the depths of degradation. He dreads to tell his wife Fanny, and gets deeper into the toils. In Fanny we have a model wife; and she it is who really saves Mark, the hero, from ruin by her influence and counsel. In the *Small House at Allington*, Trollope shows us in Lily Dale what is, I conceive, a perfect type of a good English girl: here we have a woman unmarried at her best ; in Fanny we have woman married, a woman such as Wordsworth describes—

> Nobly planned,
> To warn, to comfort, and command.

Special praise is, indeed, due to the *Small House at Allington.* This work appeared after Trollope's vain endeavour to produce a popular comic fiction in the story of *Brown, Jones, and Robinson.* It is in the *Small House at Allington* that he gives us, as observed above, his finished and lovely conception of a true typical English girl—Lily Dale. She is represented with only too true a fidelity to fact, as faithful still to a man all unworthy of a being who is not only gentle and loving, pure and good, but withal endowed with no little intellect. She has always seemed to me to be the finest in all of Trollope's female portraitures; and the whole novel is undoubtedly an admirable example of the natural and refined, with the artistic. A good deal of the work is taken up with light satire, but in many parts a note is sounded not often heard in Trollopian fiction. And how delicately does the writer paint the dawnings of the first only half-conscious quickening of a pure affection, an utterly unselfish love, as it awakens in the soul of a fair English girl as natural, as guileless, and as sweet as the very flower that names her! It has seemed to me, while reading that portion of this novel, dealing with the unfolding of a heart under the vivifying influence of an absorbing affection, that we almost feel the pulses of that vital air which breathes through every soul that fondly loves to ruin or to save. This novel throughout is a charming picture of a true woman : and who can wonder that while this story was issuing in serial form, Trollope received many letters from sympathetic admirers of his fairest creation—Lily Dale?

Now let me pass to one who all in all is one of the greatest novelists of our times, namely, the first Lord Lytton. It is remarkable that the first Lord Lytton's strong literary bent appeared very early indeed. He published a work when only fifteen years old, entitled *Ismael*, an Oriental tale ; and while at Trinity College, Cambridge, carried off the Chancellor's Prize Medal with his English poem on *Sculpture*. Early in youth he probably absorbed much material for future literary use while making pedestrian excursions very generally throughout the United Kingdom ; and after the issue of the prize poem, he published a small collection of poems—a rare book now, called *Weeds and Wild Flowers*. In 1827 he issued a metrical tale, *O'Neil, or the Rebel*, and then, I believe, his first prose fiction, *Falkland*. *Pelham, or the Adventures of a Gentleman*, came out anonymously at the end of

1827, when the author was but twenty-two years old; and though not at first well received, was ere long recognised as a novel of great merit. Then followed a far finer work, the *Disowned*, succeeded by *Devereux*, wherein the future creator of *Harold* was trying his hand at history; and in 1830 *Paul Clifford* made a marked sensation as a trenchant satire. Two years later *Eugene Aram* created a sensation as a romance of crime, and a year afterwards *Godolphin* showed that the young novelist had unexpected veins of variety in his still undeveloped genius. The *Pilgrims of the Rhine* stamped him as gifted with a singularly fecund and graceful poetic fancy; while shortly after, the publication of the *Last Days of Pompeii* and of *Rienzi* plainly revealed powers that were quite on the Walter Scott plane. Political life, statesmanship, brilliant success as a dramatist, and much solid magazine essay work occupied the succeeding years; but after *Lucretia, or the Children of Night, Harold, The Caxtons*, and *My Novel*, had appeared, it seemed as though none could venture to forecast what might be the ultimate outcome of a genius so versatile and powerful. And even here, to pass over his really fine and well-sustained epic *King Arthur*, the *Strange Story*, the occult novel mentioned in its proper place, proved a new revelation; and then was there not the *Coming Race?* Undoubtedly

the first Lord Lytton stands out wholly unrivalled
for the variety and strength of his genius; both in
the quality and the quantity of his work he occupies
a very high place even among the greatest creative
minds in the imaginative world; and if he be not
exactly first as novelist, dramatist, or poet, he has
no rival whatever, taken all in all.

I must not omit to mention Miss Charlotte Mary
Yonge, whose *Heir of Redcliffe*, *Heartsease*, the *Daisy
Chain* (a record of a number of interesting children),
the *Young Stepmother*, and other similar novels, have
for the most part plots made to enforce, in a plain
and generally sensible manner, the special doctrines
of what may be called the High Church school
of opinion.

A place of honour must be given to another
lady novelist, known at first as Miss Dinah Maria
Muloch, afterwards Mrs. Craik, who in *John Halifax, Gentleman*, produced a masterpiece of quiet,
natural, and deeply interesting domestic fiction.
As Mrs. Craik, Miss Muloch continued to write
until her death recently. With her may be classed
the late Mrs. Henry Wood, who in such novels as
*East Lynne, Mrs. Halliburton's Troubles, The Chan-
nings*, etc., has invested with a rare charm and a
living interest, the commonplace, but nevertheless
bitter to those who endure them, trials of every-
day life.

Worthy to be placed beside *John Halifax, Gentleman*, that modern epic of the true Christian life, is Mrs. Gaskell's *Wives and Daughters*. Few if any novels can vie with this in naturalness and in the evolution of really entrancing interest out of the most ordinary and matter-of-course incidents of English life. Molly Gibson, the loved and loving daughter of the country doctor, who is drawn into a second marriage by the ex-governess and curate's widow, is one of the most finished studies of girlhood in English fiction. The step-mother, Mrs. Gibson, is drawn to the life, and then the old squire in his relations to his very diverse sons is equally real. The whole reads like what it is—a most faithful transcript from nature itself. Amid so much that is most amusing here, we have ever and anon a deep full note of humanity in its more passionate phases; and there are passages, such as those where Squire Hamley grieves for his wife, and especially where he utters his exceedingly bitter cry over the death of his first-born, which draw tears from the eyes of the old as well as the young, and such tears as show through their mist some gleams of immortality and Heaven. What is most remarkable, too, about this novel is that it moves the reader without employing the machinery of anything in the least abnormal, unnatural, or even unlikely. Every incident in the story is simply what happens every day in the lives of many; and to build up a *great* novel out of such materials is surely a remarkable triumph.

That women have excelled in novel writing does not need much argument to prove. Besides two of the greatest of female novelists, George Eliot and Charlotte Brontë, how many remain, exclusive of "Ouida" and Miss Braddon, who has produced a library of more or less admirable novels, more than 150 volumes strong? Miss Braddon, I may mention, comes of a good old Cornish family; and her father, a solicitor, was once a principal contributor to the old *Sporting Magazine*. She was born in Soho Square in 1837, and at quite an early age contributed prose and verse to newspapers, and even published a volume of poetry, entitled *Garibaldi*, prior to her entering on the serious business of systematic novel writing.

Then there are Mrs. Oliphant, Miss Amelia B. and Miss Matilda B. Edwards, Annie Thomas, Frances E. Trollope, Rhoda Broughton, and very many others; while, curiously enough, Madame d'Arblay (Miss Burney), born as long ago as 1752, was, as mentioned in a previous chapter, one of the early English novelists, and produced *Evelina*, *Cecilia*, *Camilla*, and the *Wanderer*, long before the great flood of Victorian fiction began to pour forth.

Mrs. H. Lovett Cameron, author of *A Dead Past,
A Life's Mistake*, etc., Mrs. Alexander (*The Wooing
o't*, etc.), Annie Thomas, a prolific writer of fiction,
Florence Marryat, a daughter of the great naval
novelist, Mrs. Lynn Linton (*Mad Willoughby*,
etc.), Mabel Collins (*In the Flower of her Youth*),
Jean Ingelow the poet (*John Jerome*, and many
others), Mrs. George Linnæus Banks, Miss
Cummins (the *Lamplighter*, a charming American
domestic tale), Mrs. Cashel Hoey (*A Stern Chase*),
Mrs. E. Kennard (*Straight as a Die*, and many
other novels, in most of which ladies ride to hounds),
Sarah Tytler, Helen Mathers, Dora Russell (*A
Hidden Chain*), Mrs. Burnett (*Little Lord Fauntleroy*, a charming picture of a charming child), and
Edna Lyall (*Donovan, A Hardy Norseman, In the
Golden Days*, etc.), Mrs. Stewart (*Two*), and
many more, sufficiently substantiate the fact that
as novelists women occupy, indeed, a very prominent place in contemporary literature.

Charlotte Brontë claims, it need hardly be said,
a place of her own in English fiction.

To particularise: if *Jane Eyre* is the most sensational and distinctly dramatic of Charlotte Brontë's
novels, *Shirley* is not only the longest, but the
most artistic of them all. *Jane Eyre* is often
somewhat *bizarre*, and may be pithily described
as an autobiographical drama, oscillating between

11

Greek tragedy and eighteenth-century comedy, played out between Jane the governess, and Rochester her employer; and ever and anon we feel in this weird novel the hot volcanic blast of baffled passion, while the pangs of disappointed love are retailed to us in spasms. It is a great book; but *Shirley* is on a far broader canvas, and has a much more varied range of characters. *Jane Eyre* is a splendid effort; but *Shirley* is more sustained, and the pictures of the north-country curates are as good as aught in any of George Eliot's works. The book teems with unexaggerated transcripts from real life; and then while abounding in what is popularly called "domestic interest," we have in Mrs. Pryor's communings with the sick Caroline some deeply interesting colloquies on life and death. Yet these are all given in such a fluent natural manner that the reader does not think of the writer at all; and in a word what may be called the more thoughtful or ethical parts of *Shirley* are never felt to be merely slices of essays thrust in simply to air an author's whim and hinder the narrative. Both novels are extremely fine. In *Jane Eyre* Helen Burns is a marked creation; and in the touching story of her evil fate, a note is firmly struck of true pathos, while the whole of this affecting episode is, as it were, enveloped with that aureola sometimes seen in the works of the old masters.

Outside the heroine is Rochester, the hero and central figure, the pivot on which the whole of the action turns. He is undoubtedly Byronic in origin, and strikes us as a mere individualised *Lara*, *Giaour*, or *Corsair*. He is, in a word, the very man described by Byron, who, in pursuit of what he considers to be a worthy prize, let us say the woman he loves—

> Will hunt the steps of fate
> To save or slay as these require,
> Through rending steel and rolling fire.

Rochester's sardonic moods, too, are purely Byronic. Jane, on the contrary, is shaped on the Scott model, and echoes, with all her witchery and unconscious wiles, the healthy atmosphere of one who can through all the crises of life remain ever a votary of Duty, that—

> Stern daughter of the voice of God!

Jane in truth is a highly elaborated, differentiated, and much-developed version of Clara in *Marmion*. In Scott's poem Clara is not a very substantial personage; but she can sacrifice her fears and longings for a consummated happiness to an innate sense of honour and duty; as when her lover resolves to re-establish his tarnished reputation by force of arms, she is made to exclaim :—

> That reddening brow too well I know!
> Not e'en thy Clare can peace bestow
>   While falsehood stains thy name.
> Go then to fight: Clare bids thee go,
> Clare can a warrior's feelings know
>   And weep a warrior's shame.

How different this is from the ferocious sentimentality of the Byronic school, and how antithetical is the moral substratum of Jane's character to that of Rochester! In the end, too, mark how duty triumphs supremely as embodied in Jane, who in resigning everything as it seems, actually secures all.

Among novelists whose works form almost a literature of their own, is Marian Evans, and finally Mrs. Cross, popularly known as " George Eliot," whose *Scenes of Clerical Life*, appearing in *Blackwood's Magazine*, most certainly proclaimed the advent of a new and powerful novelist; and when *Adam Bede* came out in 1858, one year later, popular curiosity was widely aroused; and the next year *The Mill on the Floss*, with its masterpieces of characterisation the Tulliver family, definitely fixed the fame of the author. *Silas Marner*, the weaver of Raveloe, showed a new vein of originality; and then came *Romola*, which is usually held to be the greatest intellectual achievement of the writer. *Felix Holt the Radical, Middle*

march, and *Daniel Deronda,* succeeded; and in all
these fine novels there is highly noticeable a
great wealth of original sententious reflections,
of terse incisive observation on men, places, and
things; and, in a word, much real intellectual pith
entirely outside the art of the story, which is
usually consummate; and then the characterisation, too, is wonderfully natural and real. In a
word, these fine novels belong to permanent literature; and higher praise cannot be given. The
admirers of George Eliot are legion; and yet,
regarded as a great imaginative artist, there has
always seemed to me to be something wanting
in her work. The novelist at best, is in a
sense a poet working without the encumbrance of
rhyme or metre; and his or her supreme success
may be measured, and must ultimately be in the
final appeal, by the amount of the pure poetry
within and underlying the woof and warp of
the narrative. George Eliot, as we all know,
strove hard to achieve a first place as a poet; and
the *Spanish Gipsy, Agatha,* the *Legend of Jubal,* and
Armgart, all evince extraordinary intellectuality,
much constructive genius, and great richness of
expression. And yet, somehow, that indescribable
aroma which exhales from every true poem is absent. In truth, what the writer wanted was the
serene calm temperament of the believing soul;

for without an ample measure of *faith*, poetry
cannot exist in its highest and most far-reaching
forms. Richter says, that he would rather dwell
in the fog of superstition than in air rarefied to
nothing by the air-pump of unbelief, in which
the panting soul expires vainly gasping for breath,
—that breath which we are so pointedly told the
Creator Himself breathed into the nostrils of man.
For nearly ten years before essaying fiction, wherein lay her real vocation, Miss Evans worked hard
at metaphysics, at philosophy, and at criticism; and
then did she not translate the well-known *Leben
Jesu* of Dr. Strauss, and other books of a like
character? All this necessarily told on the future
writer, and was a fundamental bias during the
whole of her illustrious literary career. Indeed,
we have here an example of the determining power
of early reading on the mind. We can imagine if
only Miss Evans had been possessed of the gentle,
pure, believing soul of the author of *John Halifax*,
how immeasurably greater would have been her
work, and how infinitely better its influence on
the minds of all who read and admired it.

> How true it is
> A cheerful soul is what the muses love,
> A soaring spirit is their prime delight !

But how or to what can the unbelieving and
sceptical soul soar, and how can it be cheerful

with intellectual faculties quickened to preter-
natural activity, and yet with all beyond the
grave, vague or utterly blank ? It has been said
that the later years of the author of *Romola* were
darkened by the clouds that must roll over the path
that leads to infidelity; and here, as of old, we have
the familiar lesson that without true religion, all
the enjoyments of sense, all the pride and pomp of
intellect, all the intoxication of supreme fame, turn
in the end to dust, ashes, darkness, and the unspeakable despair of an ever-questioning doubt.

Yet one word more.

George Eliot covers a wide range of thought
and sentiment in her religious phases of life as
set forth in her novels. Now we have, as in Dinah
Morris, the quaint Methodist life of Wesley; and
then in Savonarola we have mediæval Catholicism
in all its energy; while again we have a true transcript of the ancient Hebrew nationality, grounded
on the solid rock of the theocratic idea. *The Mill
on the Floss*, with the old miller who always hated
"a rascal"; Tom Tulliver, who saw as a boy no
use in girls because they could not throw stones,
is admirable in its clear characterisation. In *Silas
Marner*, what true poetic and dramatic touches
abound ! as in the fine scene where after the loss
of his gold, Silas is struck by the sunshine on the
golden hair of the little child. In *Adam Bede*, too,

how firm are the portraits, and how fluent is the dialogue, each bit clearly belonging to those who utter it, and to none other!

The following fact is a striking example of the influence of fiction on some minds. A lady who had lost sight of her husband for some years, committed suicide rather suddenly by taking poison. At the inquest it was stated that some time previous to her suicide the poor woman's attention had been attracted by the following passage from George Eliot's *Romola*, which she had come across in a birthday book, and the passage appears to have excited her to action : " There are moments when our passions speak and decide for us, and we seem to stand by and wonder. They carry in them an inspiration to crime that in one instant does the work of long premeditation."

There may not have necessarily been a connection here between the perusal of this passage and the suicide referred to; but I doubt whether such a passage could be found in the novels of Mrs. Craik, or, indeed, of many other female novelists; and truly this fact accentuates my observation as to the effects on George Eliot of the entire absence of a living faith in a personal God and a personal Saviour.

One of the greatest of living novelists, in the estimation of some, is unquestionably George

Meredith, who was born in 1828. He was an orphan and a ward in Chancery, and his education was conducted in Germany, whence he drew so strong a bias and colouring for his genius. No man had a harder fight with fortune. He published early in life poems which did not sell; and who, indeed, can live on poetry, unless he be singularly favoured, as was Tennyson? It was the fantastic tales entitled the *Shaving of Shagpat* that first brought him some recognition. Then in due time came the *Ordeal of Richard Feverel;* and it was manifest that a great writer had appeared. But it is in the nature of things that greatness such as that which belongs to George Meredith should not immediately win the popularity that is accorded to a hundred inferior writers, whose novels, however, are amusing, and such as any one can read and understand without the least mental effort. George Meredith, it is interesting to note, married a daughter of the once famous Thomas Love Peacock. He subsequently took unto himself a second wife, and lived a very simple hard-working life, close to Box Hill, Surrey. But, after only two years of real happiness, he was again widowed; and since then a married daughter has shared his rural retreat. His existence is quite on the ideal poetic plane; for his pretty cottage is set in a garden on a hill-side, and in the garden is a pine-wood chalet,

wherein he is believed to do most of his thinking
and writing.   He is a very deeply read man, and
is endowed with a wonderful memory.   His novels
are richly strewn with epigrams, flashes of philosophy, and often dry bits of worldly wit and wisdom, that come only from those who think deeply.
His admirers have rapidly increased of late years ;
and it is not too much to say that in prose fiction
George Meredith is what Robert Browning is in
poetry,—and, perhaps, even more !

No doubt Mr. George Meredith is not popular
with the multitude.   He excels in dialogue and
conversation ; but it is not of the kind that helps
the story on, and his narrative faculty is not, I
think, his strong point.   He has always seemed
to me, not so much, as some declare, the greatest
living novelist, as one of the greatest of nineteenth-
century writers and profound thinkers who has
selected the novel as his final vehicle for delivering
his views and ideas to his contemporaries ; and
much of his work will undoubtedly live.

In the prelude to the *Egoist*, which is decidedly
a work of genius, Mr. George Meredith has some
truly amazing sentences.   Take a sample: "Art is
the specific.   We have little to learn of apes, and
they may be left.   The chief consideration for us
is what particular practice of Art in letters is the
best for the perusal of the book of our common

wisdom; so that with clearer minds and livelier manners we may escape, as it were, into daylight and away from a land of foghorns." And so on for some pages.

Carefully read with the context I admit that there is matter for profound thought and much metaphysical and introspective disquisition; but then one naturally wonders to find such a verbal overture to what is supposed to be a novel. Yet the same writer can pen such a noble passage as the following :—

" Is it any waste of time to write of love? The trials of life are in it, but in a narrow ring and a fierier. You may learn to know yourself through it, as you do after years of life whether you are fit to lift those that are about you, or whether you are but a cheat and a load on the backs of your fellows. The impure perishes, the inefficient languishes, the moderate comes to its autumn of decay—these are of the kind which aim at satisfaction, to die of it soon or late. The love that survives has strangled craving: it lives because it lives to nourish and succour like the heavens."

There can be no doubt that at times Mr. George Meredith, with all his unquestionable genius, is in prose nearly as obscure as Robert Browning is in much of his verse. After all, it only demonstrates the fact that the novelist is a most elastic term, comprehending, indeed, all kinds of men, from the merest story-tellers and anecdote-mongers up to the noblest poets ; and as a result, the novel has come to be almost anything, and is by turn a sermon, a political pamphlet, a scientific treatise, a poem without metres, a play to all intents and purposes, a socialistic enunciation, and a thousand and one things besides. Can we wonder, then, that in some instances, even when the novelist is a man of real genius, that story, plot, and much else that goes to make the true novel, are more or less forgotten, or, if remembered, are sadly mutilated from every true art view-point ?

Reverting to novelists who have passed from among us, no greater contrast could be found to George Meredith than that afforded by Charles Dickens. Of Dickens, indeed, so much has been written, and so eloquently written too, that it is well-nigh impossible to say aught that is new. Beginning as a humorist of unparalleled animal spirits, and having a kaleidoscopic range of fancy and wit that was simply cosmic, *Pickwick* stands forth distinct as *Don Quixote*. The three best novels of Dickens are probably *Pickwick*, *David Copperfield*, and *Little Dorrit*. But all are good ; and in the *Tale of Two Cities*, a chord of pathos is struck which shows that in the great humorist there lay a deep tragic vein and a dramatic power that was extra to his marvellous mirth-exciting faculty. Still, ascribing to Dickens the fullest meed of his unquestionable genius, it must be admitted that much of his success rested on mannerisms, on mere superficialities, and tricks, so to speak, of literary clowning, and by so much is doomed to fade out as the years pass on to new developments of life. Where Dickens has really sounded the full notes of passion and pathos, the notes will vibrate still; but there is a large quantity of caricature in his writings; and caricature cannot be permanent. This is the true reason why Dickens has not grown in fame, but rather the reverse; whereas Thackeray, who was never near him in popularity, when both were living, has steadily advanced in the estimation of good judges, and has attained to a posthumous fame surpassing that accorded to him by his contemporaries. Thackeray was wrongfully regarded as a cynic; but he was much more a Christian Horace, employing a noble prose as his vehicle; and it is surely his special glory that he is one of the very few British novelists who succeeded in delineating a gentleman.

From the contemplation of the genius of Dickens we naturally turn to that of Thackeray, of whom, indeed, it may well be said that he fully succeeded just where Dickens failed; and if there was one art in which as a novelist he excelled, it was certainly in that of delineating real ladies and gentlemen.   The *Newcomes*, for example, in the beautifully drawn character of Colonel Newcome, give us a complete full-length portrait of a true Christian gentleman; and then how true to life are the principal characters in *Vanity Fair* and *Pendennis !*

No word, perhaps, in the language has been so abused as the word *gentleman*, except its companion *lady*.   Correctly employed, it undoubtedly means a nearly perfected form of humanity, which very few novelists, indeed, have ever succeeded in even faintly delineating, or when delineated in rendering interesting.   The vast majority of so-called gentlemen simply *act* with more or less success the social part they have assumed; and as no man or woman can *always* act, now and then the ignoble and the churlish nature peeps forth.   The true gentleman, of course, *is* the gentleness he seems to be; and in him, as in the true lady, we may justly say that God and Nature meet in light.

Esmond must not be passed over, seeing that it is unquestionably one of the most highly finished and elaborated of his works.   *Esmond* is so called from the name of the hero, a chivalrous cavalier of the times of Queen Anne.   It was doubtless his deep study of that period for the purpose of making *Esmond* accurate in its historical aspects that impelled Thackeray to project a history of the reign of Anne; and certainly he knew those times about as well as they could be known by one who had not actually lived in them.

One of the curious things in many later-day novels is the way in which novelists are treated in some of them. We all know the story of Arthur Pendennis, and how he wrote *Walter Lorraine*, whence, however, we are not vouchsafed a single chapter; whereas Mr. William Black in *Madcap Violet* gives us somewhat copious extracts from the heroine's work of fiction. Then Mr. George Meredith tantalises his readers in the case of *Diana of the Crossways;* while does not the literary young lady in Mr. James Payn's *Heir of all the Ages* "dash off" her work of imagination, and become famous in a moment? Then the hero in Mr. Crawford's *The Three Fates* takes the American world by storm through the agency of a MS. which he has penned at fever heat, and which his lady-love recommends him to finish. Mr. Besant, in his fine story *All in a Garden Fair*, gives us a good sketch of authorship, and Mr. Henry James and Mr. Norris do the same. It seems reserved for Mr. George Gissing, in his typical delineation Edwin Reardon, to show us the realistic side. I cannot but think that novelists who depict imaginary genius coming, seeing, and conquering the publishers, and then making the Byronic short cut to fame, are answerable for much evil, and set many at work for whom the ultimate end is only failure and despair. It does not seem as though any good can ever be done by attempting to show what is not the case—*viz.*, that literary success is in any event an easy thing to attain. The only road thereto is one of toil, sacrifice, and endurance, even for those who have the requisite natural gifts.

One of the most realistic, and, within certain limits, graphic novelists of the day is George Gissing. His novel, *A Life's Morning*, turns on the fortunes of Wilfred Athel, an undergraduate, invalided at twenty-three, marked naturally for great things, an only son of a widowed father. He becomes attached to the governess engaged to educate the daughters of his aunt, who is the family housekeeper. To counterbalance true love, there is an heiress whom Wilfred's father desires him to marry. Emily Hood, the governess, has an unfortunate father, and in the struggle for existence in her miserable home, we have faint foreshadowings of the supreme art evinced in the *Nether World*, wherein Mr. Gissing delineates the lives of the London poor in and about Clerkenwell, London. In the *Nether World* we have a Frith-like portraiture of things as they are, combined with a Hogarthian vein of covert satire. In John Hewett, the typical British workman, a very fine character is presented. He has some money left him, and sets up as a master, but is far too good and honest to succeed. His daughter, Clara, has ambition to enter a higher life, and her struggles towards ladyhood are among the most interesting things of the kind in current fiction. Then there is a female character, a work girl, named " Clem," who is like a study from *Zola*—a piece of animalism, beautiful but entirely earthy; and other personages of this domestic drama of real contemporary domestic life are here found in great variety. The pivot of the story is Michael' Snowdon, a working man, who having amassed a fortune in Australia returns to seek out his relatives; and finding his grand-daughter, Jane, a drudge in a common lodging-house, deliberately sets to work to educate her for the practical administration of relief to the poor. The old man has philanthropic theories, and strives to make of Jane an instrument of good, and with the usual result in such cases, as human feelings, sensibilities, and affections rarely square with socialistic theories. The whole story is intensely interesting and full of incident. The description given of a Bank holiday at the Crystal Palace alluded to under " Comic and Humorous Novels " is in

12

words much after the style of Frith's Derby Day in colours. The one is as real and as vivid as the other.

Unquestionably another of the most prominent novelists of the day is Hall Caine, who in his fine work the *Bondman*, a new Icelandic saga, has struck a vibrant tragic note. It is a powerful tale of revenge, cherished by a son, who nurses the memory of his mother's wrongs, and it introduces in the penal sulphur mines of Iceland much that is wholly new to the reader. A previous work of Mr. Hall Caine's, the *Deemster*, laid in the Isle of Man, and working up in a singularly effective way the many peculiarities of Manx life and Manx customs, is, I think, a far finer work of imagination. The lives of two brothers—perfect contrasts, —are traced out; and one of them, who becomes the Bishop of Man, is as distinctly a creation as the good bishop in Victor Hugo's *Les Miserables*. Mr. Caine delineates children very finely, and he has a delicate, discriminating power of portraying women which invests his fiction with a singular charm.

Mr. Grant Allen, originally a scientist, took to fiction late in life, and has produced some striking novels, which, as may be imagined, usually rest on or exemplify some principle in science, as heredity, racial instincts, or the like. Some of Grant Allen's stories are eminently calculated to entertain the young, as in the *White Man's Foot*, wherein the story starts with the incident of Tom and Frank Hesselgrove, two young scientists, being commissioned to make observations on Mauna Loa, a famous Hawaiian volcano. Here they fall in and become acquainted with Kea, a really beautiful and refined Hawaiian girl. Kea has an uncle, a savage chief, veneered with civilisation, and retaining secretly his heathen notions. He believes that a fearful goddess—Pété—resides in the volcano, and he does not approve of the young scientists prying about the crater. It is to him utter profanity, and the more so as he is the hereditary priest of the place. To appease the enraged goddess, whose voice is heard by him in the throbbings of the burning mountain, he determines to sacrifice the innocent Kea; and it is in the determination of Frank Hesselgrove to rescue her from immolation that the story is wrought up to a very intense pitch of interest and excitement. That the newspaper spirit of haste has infected contemporary novelists is sufficiently obvious. Take one example: Mr. Grant Allen, who is certainly one of the most industrious novelists of to-day, produced *An Army Doctor's Romance* almost before the strife between the Chartered Company in South Africa and the Matabele warriors had ended. Anyhow, Lo Ben's

impis and the Maxim guns of the conquering white,
play an all-important part in a story which is not
one of the least interesting among the many
volumes of fiction that have been published by Mr.
Grant Allen.   Whether this " up to date " energy
in fiction-weaving is compatible with the higher
art of the novelist is, of course, another matter.
Mr. Grant Allen has for his latest venture issued
some poems, wherein he obtrudes his strange belief
in evolution ; and actually writes some verses to
vindicate the character of the alleged ape original
of the human race.   Why it should delight Mr.
Grant Allen to thus metrically air his own infidelity, I cannot tell; but most people will prefer
to be on " the side of the angels ".

Of late, a strong tendency has been evident to
break new ground in fiction, in out-of-the-way
foreign lands, as well as in the Colonies, of which
the *Story of an African Farm* (Olive Schreiner)
is an example.   In his novel, *A Child of Japan*,
Mr. Edward H. House lays his scene in Tokio in
the present day, and gives us in his heroine, Yone,
a good picture of female Japanese domestic life.
Yone is married to Santo, "a rough sort of animal"; and she being of noble birth and educated,
suffers accordingly, and trouble ensues when she
falls under the spell of a young American traveller,
Arthur Milton, who stays behind from his party to

study ancient Japan, but in reality because he is
so deeply interested in Yone.   She is in her way
quite a creation; and her trials and temptations,
and the way in which she bears them, form a
narrative of much power and fascination.

Place must be found for Mr. Marion Crawford,
who between 1882 and 1889 produced eleven
notable novels, of which two in particular, *Mr.
Isaacs* and *With the Immortals*, are in their respective ways remarkable.   Mr. Isaacs is an Asiatic, a
wondrous man, gifted with much that constitutes the
true hero; he is a Mohammedan, married to three
wives, who render his domestic life unbearable.
He is, however, instructed in Western ideas as to
what woman is at her best; and this instruction
is effected by his acquaintance with Katherine
Westonhaugh, a true type of the best English
girl.   The difficulties of an exceedingly delicate
situation are overcome in a masterly manner; and
among other good points in the book is the fine
exposition given to Buddhism by Ram Lal.   What
is most marked in Mr. Crawford's books is the fact
that he abounds in good writing, which is the outcome of his story, and not simply superimposed to
show how well he can write.   Sometimes, too, he
utters a deep truth in a singularly terse manner,
as when in *Dr. Claudius* he tells us, "women are
very like religion; we must take them on faith, or

go without ". Then in *Paul Patoff*, another fine novel, we have such incisive bits as this: " It is before all things important that truth should be young, lest it should not know how to be old when age comes upon it ".

Some few years ago there appeared a fiction entitled *Ideala*, which was remarkable as a philosophical study of certain mental and moral phases. Still the work did not achieve any extraordinary success at the time ; but when the author (Sarah Grand) produced, in 1893, the *Heavenly Twins*, there was quite a rush of readers for both works. The *Heavenly Twins* met with great success ; a later work of the same author's is *Our Manifold Nature*.

The late Hawley Smart was popular among many. He is well known as the author of *Bound to Win*, and *Social Sinners*. A distinctive and later work of his is the *Master of Rathkelly*. There is certainly much to hold the reader in this novel, seeing that it gives in a graphic sketch of the life of Ratcliffe Eyre of Rathkelly Castle, Ireland, a really good idea of the nature of the conflict in the sister kingdom, between landlord and tenant, between law and licence. Ratcliffe, with his spirited daughter Kate, is an interesting figure, and Kate is equally so. America sends over a member of the National Land League, and the " master" is " boycotted," and those of his tenants who remain loyal to the family are "marked" for punishment. Then there is John Saunders, whose novels, *Abel Drake's Wife, Lion in the Path* and *Bound to the Wheel* were successful in their day.

Mrs. Oliphant is essentially a novelist of much quiet power, and possessed of a pleasant style, and a clear analytical method of unfolding character, without in the least obtruding the writer on the reader. In *Lady Carr*, we have in Lady Caroline the episode of a good and somewhat ambitious woman, who as a rich widow marries the man of her early choice. This is Mr. Beaufort, a gentleman of honour and character and of ability, and yet one who makes no way, and thoroughly disappoints his wife, who imagined that when he had entire relief from worldly cares he would exert his powers; whereas he, not unnaturally, does rather less intellectually, and dawdles over the one intellectual subject in which he might have shone, until some one else actually produces the very work that he rightly knew himself competent to write !

Among Mrs. Oliphant's distinctive productions is a series of excellent novels, generically entitled *Chronicles of Carlingford;* and consisting of five distinct novels—*viz.,* the *Rector, Salem Chapel,* the *Perpetual Curate, Miss Marjoribanks,* and *Phœbe Junior.* A much more recent novel of Mrs. Oliphant's is entitled *Lady William.* It

has been aptly said that few novelists possess more
facility for reproducing, without exaggeration, social
types drawn from conventional circles.   There is
another noteworthy point; and that is that Mrs.
Oliphant possesses the rather rare faculty for indicating in a subtle way the difference that exists
between real ladies and those who are simply highly
coloured and in every respect admirable imitations
thereof.

Annie Thomas (Mrs. Pender Cudlip), author
of *Denis Donne,* and *Theo Leigh,* is in many of
her novels entertaining and sometimes exceedingly ingenious, as in *That Other Woman.*   This
story pivots on bigamy.   The hero, Phillipps-
Twisden, lives a double life; Violet, the heroine,
a delightful girl, rejects a rich baronet and marries
Phillipps.   Her father is ruined, and her mother
takes to recitation in public, and then Phillipps
conceives a mortal hatred to his mother-in-law,
and tortures his wife morally for aiding her mother,
and cuts off her allowance.   This exceedingly dis-
agreeable husband becomes infatuated with Florence, the beautiful niece of a horse-trainer, and
marries her as Twisden! Florence is "that other
woman"; and one day in the course of things social,
Violet invites Florence to afternoon tea, not dreaming of her relations with her husband.   He learns
of this, and steals from his drawing-room the

portrait of himself, determining not to appear, and hoping the matter may blow over, for Florence does not know him as he is. Violet, however, has his likeness in a locket, and missing the portrait shows it to her visitor as the likeness of her absent husband! This brings on the catastrophe.

The late Miss F. Patton-Bethune wrote several novels, *Debonnair Dick, Bachelor to the Rescue,* etc.

The novelists not exactly belonging to the first rank are indeed numerous. Taking a rapid survey we have Miss E. Everett Green, who has produced a great number and variety of novels and tales. Only a few comparatively can be enumerated here. Among these are *Church and King, In the Days of Chivalry, Lord of Kynevor, Sir Aylmer's Heir, Wars of the Roses,* and *Winning the Victory.*

Every one may not, perhaps, be aware that Mrs. Mary Cowden Clarke produced at least one novel, called the *Iron Cousin.*

Mrs. Caroline Clive, born in 1801, may be mentioned as the author of a novel which once had some vogue, and was entitled *Paul Ferrol.*

Thomas Cooper, the once famous Chartist and the author of an epic, written while imprisoned for political offences, wrote one or two novels, *Alderman Ralph,* and the *Family Feud,* which had some success. Cooper deserves mention; for,

from having been a determined infidel, he under-
went an entire change of views, and devoted much
of his time and talent to refuting the very opinions
he had once advocated.

Miss Julia Corner, born in 1815, published in
1835 her first novel entitled the *Baronet;* this was
succeeded by *Edward Castleton, Improvidence,* and
other works. Subsequently Miss Corner identified
herself with the production of some excellent edu-
cational works.

Mr. Dudley Costello, after much journalistic
work, produced from 1855 a good many fictions.
Stories from a Screen, the *Joint Stock Banker,*
the *Millionaire, Faint Heart never won Fair
Lady.*

Miss Louisa Stuart Costello began her literary
career by writing poetry; but in 1841 she put forth
a fine romance entitled the *Queen Mother,* wherein
the most prominent character is the well-known
Catherine de Medici. Another novel by this lady is
Clara Fane.

It would not be fair to omit some reference to
Pierce Egan, born in London, of Irish parentage,
in 1815; and in 1834 a student at the Royal Academy.
The young artist abandoned painting for writing,
and produced several romances: *Robin Hood, Wat
Tyler, Paul Jones,* and *Quintin Matsys,* which had
much vogue, and represents, perhaps, the high-

water mark of *London Journal* romance. George Borrow, too, should not be passed over with his *Rommany Rye*.

Then there was James Hain Friswell, who, as long ago as 1852, contributed to the *Puppet Show*, a periodical conducted by Angus B. Reach and Albert Smith. Mr. Friswell is best known as the author of the *Gentle Life*, a series of essays; but he wrote a two-volume novel, entitled *A Daughter of Eve*.

The late Lady Duffus Hardy was the author of several notable novels; among the most successful were *Paul Wynter's Sacrifice*, and *Daisy Nichol*; a posthumous novel is entitled *A Buried Sin*.

The author of *Molly Bawn*, Mrs. Hungerford, is undoubtedly a deservedly popular female novelist. In the *Honourable Mrs. Vereker*, for example, she pleads powerfully one phase of woman's constant matrimonial suffering. Mr. Vereker is a big muscular brute, who drinks and beats his wife because he is jealous of the man who feels sympathy for her unmerited sufferings. Mrs. Vereker, originally a beautiful and sensitive girl, has been sold into matrimony for an income, and the result here is extreme misery. Catastrophe succeeds catastrophe, and the story is exceedingly clever in its effects. Mrs. Hungerford, indeed, is a prolific novelist. Among her most noticeable works are *A Born Coquette Airy Fairy Lilian, April's Lady*, and *Beauty's Daugh-*

ters. But besides these, and those specially cited here, may be mentioned *Doris, Green Pleasure and Grey Grief,* an example of those peculiar titles in which Charles Reade sometimes indulged ; *Her Week's Amusement, In Durance Vile, Phyllis, Portia, Rossmoyne,* and very many others.

John Cordy Jeaffreson is another nineteenth-century novelist, born at Framlingham, 1831 ; while an undergraduate at Oxford he became a writer in newspapers. His first novel, *Crewe Rise,* appeared in 1854, and has been followed by *Olive Blake's Good Work, Live it Down, Not Dead Yet,* etc.

In Mrs. Kennard's *Matron or Maid,* the heroine, Lydia Warren, daughter of a clergyman, marries a man forty years her senior, simply for his money. He is jealous, and dying leaves her a large income, with the proviso that if she marries she shall lose it all but a mere pittance. The widow, now Mrs. Stapleton, grows into mature womanhood, hungering after affection, and meets Beaumont Dorudy, a hussar officer, handsome, weak-willed, fond of pleasure, and poor. He professes a violent love for the rich widow ; and in the issue they part, he going to India, and she to deliberately nurse her income, with a view to saving enough to enable them to marry in a few years. Beaumont is eight years younger than Lydia ; and when after five years' absence, he returns, she seems to him to

have suddenly grown old.   Lydia has managed
to accumulate forty thousand pounds in the inter-
val, and is fonder than ever of the man who, little,
if at all, touched by her devotion, deems her " old ".
It is not surprising to the reader to find a young
thing, " Dolly," an heiress, brought on the scene, and
to her the hussar loses his heart, if he really has one.
Mrs. Kennard has wrought up the character of
Lydia to a great pitch of intensity, and has produced out of a simple plot a series of very strong
situations ; but few, if any, will sympathise with
the so-called hero, who is probably sketched from
real life.   In another of Mrs. Kennard's, *A Crack
County*, there is a most amusing sketch of a very
exclusive Hunt, which is known as the Mutual
Adorationists, who resent any intruder, and deem
themselves the only gentility left in the kingdom.
To them comes one Robert Jarrett, a rich Australian, with rather uncouth manners, but a warm
heart ; and much fun is evoked out of the conster-
nation raised on his joining the Hunt in ordinary
attire, and exhibiting other tendencies to defy con-
ventionalities.

At one period, the novels of the late G. A. Law-
rence were widely read and much admired.   *Guy
Livingstone* in particular won much popularity, and
set a kind of fashion for muscular heroes.   Other
novels by the same author are *Sans Merci, Sword*

and Gown, Barren Honour, Breakspere, and *Breaking a Butterfly.*

Mrs. Macquoid has also won some favour; and in her last novel, *In an Orchard,* we have for heroine, Gabrielle Lagrine, who is a spoiled child, who marries without love, and, in a sense, only loves her husband when she has lost him.

Thomas Miller is best known as the Gainsborough basket-maker poet; but besides his poems and other works historical and relative to nature, he wrote a number of novels, among these being *Royston Gower, Fair Rosamond, Lady Jane Grey.*

Mrs. Molesworth is decidedly one of our popular novelists; and in most of her stories she delights us with her light touch, her felicity of indicating character, and the way in which she elicits from simple situations really interesting results. The *Palace in the Garden* is one of her stories; and in another, *The Third Miss Quintin,* the troubles of Ella, one of the children of Colonel St. Quintin, are recounted. She taunts her father, who has married again, with remarks as to "my *own* mother," and the resultant thought and feeling conflict with her father are thoroughly well worked out.

Miss Susannah Moodie, a sister of Miss Agnes Strickland, went to live in North America on her marriage, and produced some works of fiction, among which may be cited *Roughing it in the Bush, Flora Lindsay* and *Mark Hurdlestone.*

The Hon. Mrs. Norton, second daughter of the late Mr. Thomas Sheridan, and grand-daughter of the great Sheridan, exhibited a powerful bent for authorship at quite an early age. She wrote much verse; of her novels may be mentioned—the *Sorrows of Rosalie Stuart of Dunleath,* and *Lòst and Saved.*

The late Mr. Charles Gibbon was a fecund novelist; among his best works are *Robin Gray* and *For Lack of Gold.*

The novelist known as "Mark Rutherford" should be mentioned as the author of *Mark Rutherford's Deliverance,* the *Revolution in Tanner's Lane,* and *Miriam's Schooling.* A first of the series which he gave with the *Autobiography* is entitled *Catherine Furze,* and in this last we have a *motif* of much power. Catherine Furze is a noble woman, but the man to whom she is attracted is married. The working out of the problem is full of interest.

Walter Thornbury is mainly remembered as the writer of some stirring ballads, and of various historical and antiquarian works; but he produced some fiction. One novel, *True as Steel,* is based on Goethe's play of *Götz of Berlichingen;* and another, *Wildfire,* relates to the time of the French Revolution; while again, a third, in three volumes, *Every*

Man his own Trumpeter, is laid in the days of Louis XIV.

Mention must also be made in this section of Miss C. Tucker, who under the pen-name of " A.L.O.E." put forth many charming tales infused by a pure spirit and a high purpose. A few may be cited : *Battling with the World, Exiled in Babylon, Claudia, Cyril Ashley, Flora*, and the *Blacksmith of Boniface Lane.*

Miss Warden has written some successful novels. One of her latest is entitled *My Child and I.* This story is of the autobiographical kind ; and details the strange adventures of its heroine, Perdita, from early girlhood till a second widowhood. Mrs. Chandler Moulton also merits mention.

The *Awakening of Mary Fenwick*, by Beatrice Whitby, is a novel that certainly roused a good deal of attention. *Part of the Property* is another novel by the same writer. Mention may be made, too, of the two novels, *A Marked Man* and the *Three Miss Kings*, by Ada Cambridge; of the *End of a Life*, by Philpotts ; *Miss Maxwell's Affections* and the *Rajah's Heir*, by Richard Pryce; *Daughters of Men*, by Hannah Lynch ; *Naboth's Vineyard*, by E. Somerville ; the *Dean and his Daughter, As in a Looking-glass, Jack and Three Jills*, and *A Daughter's Sacrifice*, by F. C. Phillips ; and *Margaret Byng*, by F. C. Phillips and Percy Fendall ;

Faithful and Unfaithful, by Margaret Lee; the *Dead Man's Secret*, by J. E. Muddock, and a batch of novels by Frank Barrett, namely, the *Smuggler's Secret*, the *Sin of Olga Sassoulich*, *Found Guilty*, *Fettered for Life, Between Life and Death, A Recoiling Vengeance, John Ford and his Helpmate*, and *For Love or Honour*. One of the latest sensational stories is the *Green Carnation*, by Robert S. Hichens, which contains much social satire.

Then there is the lady who, as "John Strange Winter" (Mrs. Stannard), has achieved so much success in writing of barrack life, and, strange conjunction therewith—children. In one of her latest novels, *Buttons*, she introduces a good-natured officer having a large income, who, while on a visit at a relative's, sees and loves a pretty naturally refined nursery governess, and then discovers that she is the educated daughter of a sergeant in his own troop!

Mrs. Guyton, better known as E. J. Worboise, was exceedingly prolific as a novelist, having written over forty novels and tales. Among these may be mentioned *Amy Wilton, Grey and Gold, Married Life, Thornycroft Hall*, and *Violet Vaughan*.

The author of *Molly Bawn* is undoubtedly a gifted and sympathetic domestic chronicler. Let it not be forgotten that there is more merit in delineating vividly the ordinary, and especially the

13

conventional courses of real life, than in working
up vortices of passion, or cunningly laying the
fascinating but provoking mazes of a puzzle-plot,
whereto the key is held back to the last possible
moment. The author of *Molly Bawn* for one thing
is natural, and moreover she has a special genius
for depicting the normal phases of such life as
most of us are familiar with. She illustrates Pope's
assertion that—

> True wit is Nature to advantage dressed ;
> What oft was thought but ne'er so well expressed ;
> Something whose truth convinced at sight we find ;
> That gives us back the image of our mind.

I think *A Born Coquette* is in some ways one of
the most distinctive of her works. The sketch of
the proud but poor Irish family is racy as Lever's
similar effort, without his exaggeration and often
grotesque embellishment. Now the born coquette
is decidedly a flesh-and-blood heroine ; and her flirt-
ing, however censurable, is unquestionably natural
and interesting. There is little incident, and less
plot or invention ; but here lies the cause of this
writer's triumph; and manner and style, and especially the dialogue, are all in a state of fusion. Then
let me remark that a test of fiction is easily found in
ascertaining how far the component parts of a novel
are in fusion, or only in contact with one another.
Mosaic work may be very clever, artistic, and

ingenious, and even beautiful; but look at the variegated flower, and see how Nature fuses her tints one into another, so that each flower, for example, has a unity of its own. The greatest fictions only possess this supreme quality of being fused, not merely joined or connected part with part; and it is really this the highest art of literature that makes the charm of Shakespeare, and renders all his dramas, which are but acted and highly compressed novels, so utterly convincing in their naturalness.

A novel that has certainly excited much interest is *A Yellow Aster*, which has been likened to Mr. Meredith's *Richard Feverel*. It turns on what are represented to be the disastrous consequences of educating children on out-of-the-way methods. Probably the anonymity of the authorship had much to do with the success of the story. Some attributed the work to Olive Schreiner, and others to Mrs. Sarah Grand. The real writer is Mrs. Caffyn, the wife of an Australian doctor; she has since produced *Children of Circumstance*. There are also Mr. Colin Middleton, author of the *Fool of Destiny;* Mr. Cresswell, author of *A Precious Scamp ;* Messrs. W. Wilkins and H. Vivian, authors of the *Green Bay Tree;* and, finally, Mr. R. Dowling, author of *Tempest Driven*, etc.

Mention should be made of Mr. Murray Gilchrist, author of *Passion the Plaything*, the *Stone Dragon*, one of our latest novelists. One of the latest lady novelists is Mrs. F. A. Steel, whose novel, the *Potter's Thumb*, is much admired. Then there is that latest recruit to the army of novelists, Mr. Du Maurier, whose *Trilby*, with its pictures of Paris life, sprang into much popularity immediately after its appearance.

Reference must be made also to a story by Napoleon Bonaparte, given first to the world in *The Cosmopolitan*. The MS. was, it is said, confided by Napoleon to his uncle Cardinal Fesch, and overlooked for many years. It is an untitled fragment, and is believed to have been written in 1788, when Bonaparte, then a lieutenant of artillery, was in garrison at Auxonne, and devoting his time to a history of Corsica. The story itself is written in the first person. The hero, proceeding by ship from Leghorn to Spain, is forced by contrary winds to land on a rocky island. He is assailed during the night by two persons, one a woman in man's attire ; and then comes a story within the story, wherein the French are represented as little better than savages. Throughout this work it is notable that England is evidently the object of Napoleon's admiration, while France is as evidently the reverse. Had Walter Scott not been an author, he would have been, it is said, a soldier ; possibly had Napoleon not been a soldier he might have been an author too !

CHAPTER XII

RELIGIOUS NOVELS.

THE capability of the novel to serve as a vehicle for whatever greatly moves society, is in these days tested in a thousand ways, until, indeed, fiction has come to possess the same universal receptivity for whatever stirs contemporary life as does the newspaper itself. One of the most notable and highly suggestive results of this versatility is the evolution of the essentially religious novel ; and this certainly demonstrates, for one thing, the deep and increasing interest taken in all speculation directed towards the other life and the world to come. This species of fiction is very modern, unless we may look for the germ of it in such a piece of pure imagination as Defoe's account of the supernatural experience of Mrs. Veal, a story that was concocted to sell a heavy theological disquisition, entitled *Drelincourt on Death*. Mr. W. H. Mallock, who from essay writing drifted into fiction, has been one of the pioneers of the contemporary religious novel, which may be also regarded as the prose corollary of Tennyson's *In Memoriam;* but it was Mrs. Humphry Ward's *Robert Elsmere* that first in our own times moved the public mind so strongly as to develop a decided appetite for literature of this kind. That *Robert Elsmere* is a clever novel is beyond question; but it seems strange that so careful and thoughtful a writer as Mrs. Humphry Ward should have quite overlooked, as it seems, the fact that Robert Elsmere in his experiences of scepticism, and when under the influence of the unbeliever Roger Wendover, never attempts to argue back, or to defend, any of the positions which, as a priest, he was bound, at least, to attempt to vindicate. It is curious, too, that Robert, who is otherwise described as being highly intellectual, and exceedingly well read, should be delineated as yielding up all his faith in supernatural Christianity, consequent on doubt as to the authenticity of Daniel. It might be imagined that so determined an onslaught on the Christian Religion, regarded as a Divine Revelation, would have, at least, been fortified by some kind of argumentative dialogue: but in truth nothing of the kind is attempted, and poor weak Robert surrenders his faith the very moment that the sneering, sceptical, satirical squire points his dogmatic denials at him. In fact, this is on analysis the flaw of the book from an impartial view-point; besides, the writer also naturally lays herself open to the insinuation that she omitted the argumentative portion, simply from inability that way to demolish Christianity—a conclusion to which all believers must naturally come. Surely a more candid member of the higher criticism would have avoided the manifest error, in such a fiction as *Robert Elsmere*, of allowing the hero to yield immediately to arguments of which, to the reader at all events, little is presented beyond dogmatic assertions, and sneers at what the writer conceived to be the errors in sundry Bible Dictionaries. Then, again, is there any escaping the conclusion that Robert Elsmere is really made to appear a greater success, so far as practical life goes, when in his orthodox, than when in his heterodox intellectual garb? It is certain that Catherine, and Newcome the High Churchman, remain to the end stronger and more effective characters by far than does the weak and yielding Robert Elsmere.

Another important fact in relation to the obvious reply to such objections as are raised in *Robert Elsmere* is this: Many readers are entirely unprovided with the material for even a single refutation of the scepticism which is now so generally interwoven with the very tissue of some of the popular religious novels of the day. How many ordinary

readers know, for example, that Irenæus is one of
the most important living links between Christ as
He was on earth, and the Church founded on His
life ? Well, it is a fact that Irenæus actually
quotes the four Gospels by the names of Matthew,
Mark, Luke, and John.   Then Irenæus was personally acquainted with Polycarp, who, it is on un-
doubted record, related to Irenæus certain conver-
sations that he had held with St. John.   Not only
with St. John, let us observe, but with others who
had actually seen the Saviour, and who had, moreover, witnessed some of His miracles.

What, indeed, can well be expected in days at
once demócratic and secular ?   Everywhere the
forces of ultra-Liberalism are at work divorcing the
masses from the ancient beliefs ; and the very
courses of contemporary education and of culture
are mostly directed towards material issues.
Science arrogates to itself an ever-increasing share
in every scheme of popular training ; and the results are painfully palpable all around us.   Yet in
a measure, this state of things was anticipated by
not a few thinkers of the past ; and one cannot
refrain from remembering how Wordsworth wrote
many years ago :—

Oft have I seen, ere time had ploughed my cheek,
Matrons and sires—who, punctual to the call
Of their loved Church, on fast or festival
Through the long year the house of prayer would seek

By Christmas snows, by visitation bleak
Of Easter winds, unscared, from hut and hall,
They came to lowly bench or sculptured stall
But with one fervour of devotion meek.
I see the places where they once were known,
And ask, surrounded e'en by kneeling crowds,
Is ancient piety for ever flown ?
Alas ! even then they seemed like fleecy clouds
That struggling through the western sky, have won
Their pensive light from a departed sun !

Warnings of the times are numerous and serious. On 4th February, 1894, for example, in Paris there was a celebration of what is termed civil baptisms. Many municipal authorities were present, and full 1500 persons in all. The ceremony was generally a mockery of religion, substituting nature for faith, and declaring that the function of the promoters of this ghastly parody of one of the most solemn and affecting offices of Christianity was simply to wean children from false doctrines that numb the heart and warp the mind ! Obviously believers in revealed religion may reasonably take this warning, and remember that the Church of which they are necessarily the champions, needs sword as well as shield to meet such abominations. The idea of warping infants into blank and despairing atheism is peculiarly horrible ; and ought undoubtedly to be held as a crime, and punished as such. But to return to our subject. Religious novels so called differ widely. One by Constance Howell,

entitled *A More Excellent Way*, has for its heroine,
Agatha, the wife of a collector in India, named
Hathaway, who has nothing in common with her,
their marriage having been one of "convenience".
He is described as being startled by finding his wife
is a free-thinker; he confesses to being one himself,
but still insists on their little boy being brought up
in the usual way. "Christianity," he remarks,
"does good—it has an important influence;" and
he confides to his wife that in his opinion, boys
when grown up, must throw off the trammels of
religion, but girls are to keep them for ever! It
is, observes this exemplary gentleman, "women
who throng the churches, and *they* keep society together." Agatha is shocked at this view; she is
a Radical, as her husband is a Conservative, and
flatly refuses to teach her boy aught of religion.
The father is firm, and the boy goes to school, but
practically the mother devotes her life and her
means to propagating infidelity, and eventually
persuades her son to declare himself to be an
atheist! Obviously such a "situation" is against
nature; for the misguided woman is described as
weeping tears of joy and smiling ecstatically when
her son agrees with her that no future exists for
man beyond the grave! The special pleading of
the book, and the puppet-like character of the
dramatis personæ, need not be insisted on here. All

the free-thinkers in the story are, as it were, angels of light ; and all the Christians are hypocrites or worse. We have here black *v.* white, and, perhaps, in producing this novel, the author has really done good service to the very religion she affects to despise.

There is one fact that is, I think, very remarkable and most suggestive, when we come to consider the position, the development, and the prevailing character and influence of the contemporary religious novel. It is that, allowing for a few exceptions, I believe, a very few exceptions, it is only comparatively of late that novelists have deliberately set to work to sap away the faith of their readers in the truth of revealed religion. No doubt, in what it pleases advanced thinkers to call "bad old times" there were wicked fictions issued, there were novels of a highly vicious tendency; but such never were mounted on the topmost waves of critical commendation, such novels were never really tolerated by cultured people where they circulated; it was felt that shame attached to their possessors, and still more to their perusal, and they were universally regarded as pernicious forms of degraded literature. Our forefathers in this matter did not glory in what was universally known to be a shame. It has been apparently reserved for the latter nineteenth century to

exhibit the intellectual phenomena of some of the
best and brightest intellects of the day being devoted to the dismal as well as the awful task of
trying to deprive men and women of the only form
of faith that is of the smallest service in facing the
hour of death.   The "bad old days," as they have
been called, had a vicious fiction, but virtually not
a deliberately irreligious type of novel; and now we
have not only as vicious a fiction where it has been ·
influenced by French naturalistic methods, but an
infidel fiction, whereon has been lavished a great
wealth of able argument, of ingenious special
pleading, and of rhetoric and eloquence.   In such
old-time novels as he was permitted to appear
in at all, the atheist was held up to scorn and
obloquy, and was treated as the villain of the
melodrama; now, however, he is made the interesting hero, and when he is at his very worst,
and most deserving of our deepest reprobation,
the angel of Christian mercy is invoked to cover
him with the wings of a charity for which he has
not the smallest valid claim.   Doubtless, some
superficial novelists have caught the taint of infidelity from the way in which the accredited
ministers of Christianity usually pose on the
stage; and this is partly due probably to the
mistaken action of those who imagine that bringing the Church as some try to do to the stage,

is the same as bringing the stage to the Church; no two things obviously could differ more completely.

At first to some these remarks will, perhaps, sound harsh and too sweeping; but on consideration it will appear that it is not so. If Christianity is a divinely revealed religion, then obviously those who assail it subtly and under cover of the most admittedly innocent form of mental recreation must merit the greater condemnation on the great day of reckoning which comes at length to every son and daughter of Adam.

Yet a word more on *Robert Elsmere*. In a work published in 1890 by Mr. S. B. G. M'Kinney, called the *Abolition of Suffering*, the following passage occurs: "The leading teachers of Christianity come forth fully armed to resist the onslaught of a book like *Robert Elsmere*. . . . How can a scientific student respect religious belief that could be shaken by a book which is founded on ignorance of the meaning of religion, and which proves nothing except that a clever woman is incapable of original reasoning? The citadel that shakes when a drunken man falls against it ought at once to be demolished; and the ship that hoists signals of distress for fear of collision with a jelly fish cannot be destroyed too soon." The same writer dealing with the question of agnosticism says: "The agnostic who denies the truth of revelation, and refuses to study carefully the evidence in its favour, is like the captain to whom is given a chart to guide him safely through unknown shoals, but who closes his eyes and objects to look at the chart because he cannot see the opening of his course through the breakers. . . . An agnostic in religion approaches very near to the fool who says in his heart that there is no God; and he tries to throw away the gift that he has, like a soldier who would throw away his sword because it will not serve him as a boat in crossing a river."

Miss Corelli is the writer of a three-volume novel or romance entitled *Barabbas; a Dream of the World's Tragedy*. This work, on its appearance, evoked much adverse criticism. A publisher's announcement, indeed, said : " Miss Corelli's new romance has been received with much disapprobation by the secular papers, and with warm welcome by the religious papers. By the former she has been accused of blasphemy and bad taste; by the latter, 'the dignity of the conception' and the 'elevating and devout character' of the book have been praised." For one thing in this work, Miss Corelli draws some most extraordinary conclusions for her entirely original reading of the Gospels. More reverent critics apparently than those speaking through the medium of the accredited Christian press, have expressed a firm conviction that there are certain subjects which ought never to be made use of in fiction. The overpowering objections to the innately profane Passion plays naturally apply to books of this kind with equal force.

It were well, indeed, if readers of anti-Christian novels were better informed than they usually are as to the real facts of the case, when subtle attacks on revealed religion are cunningly worked into the very tissue of more or less fascinating fiction. Thus, take only one thing—miracles—whereon so much doubt is cast in some contemporary "religious" novels. How many ordinary readers have ever given any real study to this momentous subject? In this connection I may cite a passage from a book entitled the *Mystery of God*, by T. Vincent Tymms, wherein occurs a complete answer to, indeed a thorough refutation of, Hume's argument in his famous essay designed to prove that no evidence could render a miracle credible. Now this argument, as Mr. Tymms points out, contains a latent and fatal fallacy. Hume states that his argument was suggested by perusing Tillotson's refutation of the doctrine of transubstantiation in the Lord's Supper. Tillotson argued simply that the evidence of our senses is stronger than any other testimony. Now Hume did not apparently perceive that the line of reasoning which was valid for Tillotson's purpose was useless for his own. The dogma of the real presence actually contradicts the evidence of our senses; but how is it with the miracles of the Bible? Do they contradict human sense? Were the wedding guests at Cana asked to "imagine" that they drank wine, when their senses informed them that they were quaffing water? And thus with every Bible miracle. But then Hume declared that miracles could not be credible because they were contrary to experience. Mr. Tymms pertinently asks, to whose experience? Of course to Mr. Hume's; but then we claim that although contrary to Mr. Hume's experience it was not contrary to the experience of very many who lived in the days of Christ.

Readers of religious novels should certainly know something as to the so-called evidences for evolution. It is worthy of note, that about the close of 1893 Sir William Dawson published, after fifty years of controversy, what he calls a closing deliverance, being *Some Salient Points in the Science of the Earth ;* wherein hardly any geological points are left unnoticed, while in relation to each he attacks and argumentatively routs the most advanced of scientific evolutionists. Palæontology (the science of fossil remains of animals now extinct) furnishes, he shows us, no evidence of the alleged transformation of one species into another ; and he proceeds to demonstrate that the burden of its real testimony is to establish the fact that species came in *per saltum*, and not by any slow and graduated process. This, of course, is in direct harmony with the Bible. Any way, this volume is a powerful indictment of some of the favourite positions of the evolutionists, and it shows clearly how much assumption and fallacy underlie their studied assaults on the impregnable rock of revealed religion.

It is not only Sir William Dawson, however, who directly challenges Darwinianism, and goes to demonstrate the purely speculative nature of the much-vaunted theory of evolution. The illustrious M. de Quatrefages is one of the first of French, or rather of European, scientists : and in his work entitled *Emulators of Darwin* he very fully establishes the contention that the beginnings of life upon the earth remain an impenetrable mystery. He declares that the animal or the vegetable is, each in its turn, an entity, like any simple body in chemistry : and in this he obviously corresponds very closely with the plain matter-of-fact statement in the Divine record of Genesis.

In such a novel as *A Lonely Life,* by the author of *Wise as a Serpent,* we have a type of religious novel of a very different character from *Robert*

14

Elsmere and similar productions. Harold Seton, a gifted, cultured, high-spirited young man, finding there is a doubt as to his legitimacy, practically hands over everything he has inherited to his cousin, the next of kin, and until the doubt is cleared up, works as a celibate clergyman among the worst of the poor. He lives and denies himself the gratification from a pure sense of duty, and altogether leaves behind the record of a noble life of self-sacrifice, during which he brings one terrible worldling to a true sense of religion. Such a book is in great contrast to *Robert Elsmere*, and teaches quite another sort of lesson.

In *Sheba*, by "Rita," we have, on the contrary, very visible marks also of the influence of *Robert Elsmere*. Sheba has disquisitions with Hex, her brother, on matters theological, and finds stumbling-blocks in the Old Testament. It seems incredible that the true meaning of the hardening the heart of Pharaoh should not be better understood, and that any writer should talk of "poor Pharaoh," as though he had been terribly wronged and cruelly used! Any Sunday School teacher could tell that the "hardening" was by Pharaoh himself, the prerogative of his own proud self-will resulting from being left to the influence of his own self-made character. Then again, we are asked, what harm did Cain do that his sacrifice should be rejected; and was it not better to offer the fruits of the earth, rather than kill lambs? Again, any Sunday School teacher could answer that Cain's sin was that of self-sufficiency and pride; he would not, as he deemed it, abase himself, like Abel, to the level of a guilty creature requiring an atonement or sacrifice. A reference to Hebrews xi. would have reminded Sheba that by faith it was that Abel offered more excellent sacrifice than Cain, by which he obtained witness that he was righteous. However, it must be remembered that in all these theological novels, the writers seem to entirely forget the fundamental principles of true liberalism, which obliges us as controversialists to inquire most carefully what are the answers to our destructive criticism before we can consistently arrive at a conclusion.

In antithesis to these anti-Christian novels may be mentioned a story entitled *Captain Lobe* by John Low, which is really a novel of the Salvation Army, unique of its kind, and laid in Slumdon. Captain Lobe, the hero, has but a pound a week; he spends half on himself and dispenses the rest in charity. The heroine, Ruth, devotes herself likewise to the cause of the unrefined, ignorant, and for the greater part unbelieving poor; and altogether, as an experiment in fiction, this story of the Salvation Army is noticeable.

In regard, indeed, to the religious novel or
romance, which is so popular a form of fiction
now-a-days, it is difficult, perhaps, to define, were
one so inclined, what should be its due limits.   It
has been said that nothing is sacred to a sapper,
to this might well be added or a latter-day nineteenth-century religious novelist.   Certainly, it
would appear, however, that there are some
bounds that should not be overstepped, although
it is obviously very difficult to draw the exact line.
In 1891 there was issued anonymously a work, of a
very decided religious character, entitled the *Christ
that is to be : a Latter-day Romance*.   This singular
novel is cast in autobiographical mould, and the
narrator is supposed to be living in the year
2100 A.D., when it is represented that socialistic
ideas have triumphed in Europe, that China has
become a great active power, that England has
lost her colonies, and has no territory beyond her
own geographical boundaries, that greater London
has resolved itself into the original villages, which
had been fused together, and finally that a belief in
the spiritual has faded out.   In short, the book is
an attempt at a representation of what the successful democracy of the West might well become.   It
is, though the writer does not say so much, a fair
picture of a materialism that is likely enough to
occur as a result of secular national education and

of the substitution of physics for ethics in general culture,—a condition of things that could never come to pass, by the way, if only on

> Each Board School roof
> Had ever stood the conquering Cross of Christ.

There is a fairly interesting vein of love story, mingled with the social, political, and religious complications and disquisitions of the writer; and an endeavour is made to depict the way in which an all-sufficient civilisation, all-sufficient in its own boundless conceit, would receive the second Advent. Here I pause: to my mind the working out of the romance with all its evident merits, transcends the proper functions of any writer; and doubtless many who have read this remarkable romance have felt that it decidedly oversteps what ought to be bounds beyond which the religious novelist ought not to go. The intention of the *Christ that is to be* is doubtless admirable; and just fault cannot well be found with any particular part, although the whole conception is such as can hardly fail to communicate a painful shock to those who hold that certain things are too sacred for any kind of artistic treatment in the guise of fiction. Of *Ben Hur, or the Prince of the House of David,* and some similar works, it is needless to write in detail, as they are so widely known.

CHAPTER XIII

NOVELS OF BUSINESS LIFE.

COMMERCIAL fiction—if we may so call it—is of comparatively recent origin. Time was—and not so very long back—when the introduction of the business element into a novel, unless in a very hazy and indirect allusive way, would have been a prime obstacle to publication; and even if a publisher could have been found, the libraries would have refused to subscribe. The fiction heroes of old, like a well-known character in one of Trollope's novels, never come into immediate contact with money; and "Ouida's" heroes, on whom a golden shower seems perpetually falling, or who by antithesis have nothing at all, were the types that best suited the times. Trade, in fact, was regarded as utterly sordid, and in the concrete as little less than dishonourable; and when its representatives were permitted to appear on the stage of the fictionist, it was generally to hold them up to scorn and ridicule. The debtor was the refined and proud gentleman, and the creditor was the knave; and the

Shakespearian motto, " Base is the slave that pays," was usually carried out very exactly in the case of the impecunious hero, who sought to repair his shattered fortunes by marrying some heiress. Now, indeed, all this is quite changed, and our novels often deal with trade in its most familiar and even commonplace forms. To the stilted artificial sentiment of a former day, business seemed quite incompatible with any form of imaginative work; and readers felt surprised when even a once popular poet ventured to remind them that commerce brought

> Into the public walk
> The busy merchant, the big warehouse built,
> Raised the strong crane, choked up the loaded street
> With foreign plenty.

All this sounded to most as quite coarse and vulgar; and it was long ere common-sense prevailed, and writers of fiction began to perceive how much might be made out of the myriad phases of the business life.

Among those who have wrought with marked success in this direction is Mrs. Riddell, who has produced a series of excellent novels, all dealing with business, such as *George Geith*, *Too Much Alone*, *City and Suburb*, and many others, wherein are to be found some clear and instructive delineations of struggling men of business.

In *Too Much Alone* we have the pathetic history

of a manufacturing chemist—a man of real ability, who virtually sacrifices his wife and child to a devouring ambition to succeed in his business and achieve fortune.

In the *Race for Wealth* will be found one of the best descriptions extant of the way in which certain manufacturing chemists meet the demand that unfortunately exists—fostered by competitive cheapness—for various forms of adulterated goods. This novel, too, contains, in the delineation of the wife of the hero, one of the most touching, beautiful, and natural pictures in fiction, of a pure, good, and all-sacrificing woman. Moreover, a conspicuous merit of this, and of most of the novels of Mrs. Riddell, is the fact that effects are not sought at the expense of probability. The reader is never outraged as to his common-sense by the introduction of unlikely incidents; and yet, those actually given are to the full as interesting and fresh as any of the outrageous inventions forced upon readers by novelists who do not know how to render the commonplace deeply interesting.

Very beautiful, too, in conception, and highly finished in detail, is *Far above Rubies*, wherein Mrs. Riddell shows with a firm touch how it is possible for an ordinary commonplace woman, a conventional "lady" of the times, who knows nought of evil or passion except by hearsay, to rise to the occasion of real trials in life, and to develop in a manner totally unexpected, and yet absolutely natural, devotion and love, and a loyalty to a weak selfish husband, which marks her out as a true heroine, and yet one devoid of even a touch of the unreal or the melodramatic.

Very much may be learned from Mrs. Riddell's books of city and factory life. They deal largely with actual existence in the counting-house, the laboratory, and the factory; and they are remarkable for the fidelity of their details to actual fact.

Another novelist who has very successfully followed this line of writing is Mr. F. W. Robinson, who, in many of his realistic novels, affords us a good insight into the ways in which money is actually made, and commercial success achieved. We learn from his plain matter-of-fact books the way whereby most of his characters earn their living—a thing that never would have been tolerated in the palmy days of the three-volume "fashionable" novel, which almost always included a ball, an elopement, a duel, and a grand wedding, in the concluding chapter.

In a very meritorious novel, entitled *Mattie, a Stray*, Mr. Robinson opens his story in a stationer's shop, and business in a variety of practical forms is the prevailing theme of the writer. Doubtless one cause that has combined to bring about this revolution in fiction lies in the inordinate growth of our cities, the continual decay of rural life, and the fading away of the grandeur and glory of the old territorial families. Business has flowed like a flood all over the land, and no longer can it be justly said that consummate men of business are almost as rare as poets. All classes of men are more or less engaged in some form of business ; and when even the aristocracy and the clergy are to be found directing the operations of industry, it is no wonder that the writer of fiction should take up a theme which has rather come to him than he to it.

There is, undoubtedly, a very great future for commercial fiction ; and no opportunity can be more tempting, perhaps, than this, for writers who have special ideas and views on political economy and on socialism in all its varied and perplexing forms. The great business novels—books to move men, and possibly to move the legislator too— belong to the future ; but that future is—if I mistake not—by no means distant.

CHAPTER XIV

NOVELS OF SCHOOL AND COLLEGE LIFE, AND FICTION FOR THE YOUNG.

THE advent of the now well-known book *Tom Brown's School Days* marks a distinct epoch in literature for boys, in opposition to the often mawkish stuff provided for them, which was, in too many cases, simply a series of detested lessons clumsily disguised as a story. Thomas Hughes was himself educated at Rugby under the famous Dr. Arnold; and in describing the troubles and trials of "Tom Brown," he produced a masterpiece, because he really wrote from fact and observation, and thus imparted a reality to his vivid pictures of school life as it was then, which was at once recognised as a personal transcript.

Thomas Hughes has not been a very prolific writer. He followed up his great success of *Tom Brown's School Days* by publishing *The Scouring of the White Horse*, referring, so far as the horse is concerned, to the well-known ensign of the Kentish Saxons; and then he put forth *Tom Brown at*

Oxford, wherein we have what may be called the mental history of the hero, together with excellent sketches of college life. *Tom Brown*, whether at school or college, is full of instruction as well as of entertainment for all classes of readers, and things are to be learned from these works which can hardly be found elsewhere. No doubt, some of the incidents are revolting enough, as in the terrible case of the roasting of a boy; but surely if such appalling savagery could be, it is better that it should be revealed in all its cruelty, shame, and utterly abominable character.

How much wisdom, homely but strong, simple and true, is there not in *Tom Brown?* Take the advice given by the father to his son at the outset: "Now, Tom, my boy," said the squire, "remember you are going at your own request to be chucked into this great school like a young bear, with all your troubles before you. . . . If schools are what they were in my time, you'll see a great many cruel blackguard things done, and hear a deal of foul bad talk. You tell the truth, keep a brave and kind heart, and never listen to or say anything you wouldn't have your mother or your sister hear, and you'll never feel ashamed to come home, or me to see you." Surely we have here quite an essence of Christian ethics, packed up in plain matter-of-fact every-day speech.

Verdant Green by "Cuthbert Bede" (the Rev. Ed. Bradley) gives a series of pictures of life at Oxford; but these, inclining so much to caricature, have been included under the section of "Comic and Humorous Fiction," whereto they more properly belong.

Among recent writers of works based on school life is Mr. Talbot Baines Reed, who, in a thick volume of nearly 500 pages, gives a story of school and city life, under the title of *My Friend Smith.* Mr. Reed previously wrote stories of school life, one being the *Fifth Form at St. Dominic's ;* and the value of these books is undoubtedly considerable, when we remember that in these quick-moving and restless times, from town and village all over the United Kingdom, youths by the thousand are cast adrift from home and family influence, and exposed to a thousand subtle temptations. Hence, books giving fairly accurate transcripts of life as it is, have an evident utility beyond the pleasure they impart to their readers. The story referred to above is told by Master Freddy Botchelor, an orphan, who is at first, at all events, a "bad boy," and hence, no doubt, much more interesting to the reader than if he were a faultless lamb. His adventures at Stonebridge School are very amusing. The schoolmistress is a tyrant, and the boys rebel; the details thereof being on the whole fresh, and not stale repetitions of what may be found in other works of this type. The after business life of the boy is full of incident and excitement too, and suggests what a wide and attractive field there is for the pen of the fictionist in dealing with the thousand and one phases of mercantile life.

But beyond what may be called the practical novel of boyhood and youth, of school and college, of shop or counting house, we have now quite a somewhat novel kind of fiction based on adventure and travel. Thus it may be truly said that if more is now exacted from the young of both sexes than has been the case before, a vast multiplication of pleasures for both young readers, more especially in the matter of fiction, has taken place. Time was when for boys and girls books were indeed limited in number and circumscribed in character; and even *Robinson Crusoe*, the *Pilgrim's Progress*, and *Sandford and Merton*, lose something of their charms and grow monotonous when there are no other books to contrast with them. Miss Edgeworth came, indeed, to the rescue with various tales for the young; and very good some of these are, but their range is very limited and their colouring pale beside what was to come a generation later; while now we have veritably a library of literature, fact and fancy, fun and frolic, mirth and marvel, which practically makes the

young reader free of the whole world and a den-
izen in imagination of some delightful region not
to be found in any of our school geographies or
maps terrestrial or celestial.   It is the literature
of pleasure, of absolute recreation, often cunningly
compounded with much that is deeply instructive
and widely informatory, but still the main intent
and purpose is just amusement; and rich and
rare and kaleidoscopic in variation are the literary treats now provided for the young readers of
the age.   Truly, to thousands, the opening of
the volume is, indeed, like standing on the enchanted carpets mentioned in the Arab legend,
which immediately wafted the fortunate individual who did so off to some paradisaical region
of continuous pleasure.   A somewhat neglected
writer, describing a house of ideal joy, says :—

> No sun is there; the air itself is light
> And life; a rainbow spans it like a crown
> Of tearless glory; and the forest trees
> Sweep round it in a belt of living green.
> . . . Sound has but one voice,
> And that is joyous song; sight but one object,
> And that is happiness.

To this fine poetic picture of an ideal bliss we
must add the most vivid panoramic recurrence of
incidents and episodes and the long processional
splendours of man's greatest achievements which

go to swell the chronicles of history, adventure, of heroism and devotion; and then we may have an approximate idea of the nature of our current recreative literature for young folks.

There is Mr. Rider Haggard, for example, who has such fascinating episodes to lay before his young readers. *King Solomon's Mines* and other of his romances are well known, but *Maiwa's Revenge* is perhaps less generally familiar. This is a tale of a tremendous feud between two South African chiefs, Nala and Wambe, the latter described as the most cruel chief in that part of Africa. Allan Quatermain goes on Wambe's territory to hunt elephants. One of Wambe's wives comes to him with a warning letter written on a leaf, telling him to fly, as Wambe is sending an impi (a Zulu regiment) after him. This letter emanates from an unfortunate Englishman, John Every, who is enslaved among the natives. Wambe is a terrible man—almost a fiend—he has a trap in which he tortures his captives, and he slays his own children for fear they should grow up and depose him. Terrific fights ensue, and in the issue Quatermain succeeds in rescuing John Every. A late novel of Mr. Haggard's is *The People of the Mist*.

Then there is that very voluminous writer for boys, Mr. R. M. Ballantyne, whose books are legion, including *Martin Rantes, Wild Man of the West, Young Fur Traders, The Dog Crusoe,* etc. One of the later, entitled *Blown to Bits, or the Lonely Man of Rakata,* deals with the eastern archipelago, and introduces the appalling volcanic eruption in Krakatoa, in 1883. The "lonely man" is a kind of scientific hermit who lives almost over a volcano, and is ever grieving for his daughter carried off by pirates. The hero, Nigel Roy, has some wonderful adventures, and his companion Moses, a negro, is a most amusing fellow, who relieves the more tragic portions of the narrative. In the *Middy and the Moors,* we have a striking account of the adventures of a young middy, who, going boylike for a long solitary row on the Mediterranean, is swept out to sea, and eventually run down by an Algerian pirate.

Another writer of fiction of this type is Dr. Gordon Stables. In his *Wild Life in the Land of the Giants,* we have a tale of two Cornish brothers, who, taking to the sea as a profession, eventually find themselves in Patagonia. The brothers are besieged in a little citadel of their own construction by a horde of awful savages, for we are told that the Fuegian Indian has but one object in the world, and but one motto—kill and eat!

Of a different type to these "fighting" stories are some of the tales for the young by Mr. G.

Manville Fenn.   One of these, and a typical story
it is, is *Quicksilver, or the Boy with no Skid to his
Wheel.*   In this tale we have a Dr. Grayson, who
has a very delightful daughter, much wealth and
philanthropy, and a singular hobby.   It is, that you
can make what you will of a boy if you take him
in hand early enough.   Dr. Grayson, with a view
to substantiating his theory, visits the Union, and
picks out thence one described as being the very
worst boy in the place.   This lad the doctor adopts;
and it may be imagined that the results of the
experiment are frequently intensely comic.   The
late W. G. Kingston wrote a library of boys'
stories; then there are A. R. Hope (Moncrieff),
who began with a book about *Dominies,* and Farrar
with the Neronian romance *From Dark to Dawn.*

Then there is Mr. G. A. Henty, who has produced
numerous captivating fictions for boys and girls.
One of these semi-historical tales is called the *Cat
of Bubastes,* and gives us much insight into the
every-day life of the ancient Egyptians.   Amuba,
a Prince of the Rebu nation, is, after a great battle,
taken captive by the Egyptians, together with his
faithful charioteer Jethro, and both are borne from
their home on the Caspian Sea, into the then
mighty and highly civilised land of the mystic Nile.
Here the captives are assigned to Ameres, an Egyptian priest; but a pleasant servitude is brought to a

close and a crisis by the accidental killing of a sacred cat. The descriptions given of Thebes, and of the manners and customs of the inhabitants, are not only very interesting, but based on fact ; and from these pages much may be learned of the life of the ancient Egyptians.

As an entire contrast to this, I may cite a recent romance of Japan, entitled the *Curse of Koshua*, by the Hon. Lewis Wingfield.   Here we have a chronicle of the Hojo family, who rose in the fourteenth century to power, and then fell with an appalling crash.   The opening passage tells us that this feudal story of the land of the Rising Sun is a long chronicle of blood and tears, of rapine and vendetta, whence, at intervals, there streams forth a gleam of splendid heroism, of holy sacrifice, and of pure love.   The love of the armourer Sanjo for the tall and pale O'Tei is well told, and the charm of the novel lies in its utter strangeness.   We read of Feudalism, and find it entirely unlike in form what is understood by the term ; but, probing beneath the surface, we can soon perceive how strong a resemblance there was morally in many ways between the haughty Japanese noble and the Norman feudal chief.

While on this subject of chivalry, one must remember Mr. Andrew Lang, a charming writer in many styles, and a worker of many veins of literature. One of his very pretty romantic fictions is the *Gold of Fairnilee*. The story begins in the old Scotch house where Randal, the hero of this mediæval tale, was born. The child's father is described as having fallen on the fatal field of Flodden; and Lady Ker, Randal's mother, not unnaturally hates the English. She, however, is moved to pity by a beautiful little girl who has been somehow mixed up with the spoil carried off by Lady Ker's retainers, and thereby we have a pretty thread of romance to disentangle. Randal is lost, and cannot be found, although he is sought far and near; down in Yetholine among the gipsies, and across the Eden in merry Carlisle, and all through the land debatable, and far down Tweed. Poor Lady Ker's hair turns white; and at last, after years, Randal returns, and there is joy at Fairnilee. Randal, however, has had experiences of fairyland, something like bonny Kilmeny in James Hogg's beautiful metrical legends, the *Queen's Wake*.

One of the most remarkable features in the development of fiction during the last few years of the period 1880-1893 has been undoubtedly the increasing popularity of the short story, which is a novel of action usually compressed into its narrowest limits. I say of action, but of course the action may be of the psychical character, although in general these exercises of ingenuity in condensing fiction commonly concern themselves mainly with the material side of things.

A writer in the London *Echo* of 3rd October, 1893, says:—

"Our works of fiction have been getting briefer and briefer.   Shilling 'shockers' for the million have led to dainty eighteenpenny 'pseudonyms' for the cultured public; and the success of these essays in 'psychology by epigram' has led to an even more complete confinement of the three-volume novel to the lady patrons of the circulating libraries.   For we are nearing the apotheosis of the short story, and short stories must be published in single-volume form."

The same writer goes on to remark:—

"Older writers, like Mr. George Meredith, Mr. R. D. Blackmore (old in spirit), or Mrs. Oliphant, and romancists like Mr. Hall Caine, Mr. Buchanan, and Mr. Rider Haggard, have avoided the temptation, because the form is foreign altogether to their method, while Messrs. Walter Besant and James Payn have only published their inferior work in the shape of novelettes.   But many of the younger generation have entirely abandoned themselves to this style of fiction. Chief among *les jeunes* stands Mr. Robert Louis Stevenson, and despite the literary perfection of

Catriona and the *Master of Ballantrae*, we are inclined to think *Thrawn Janet* and its fellow stories contain his most suggestive work. Another exquisite stylist, Mr. Henry James, also shows at his best in these miniatures. Side by side with these two we set Mr. Hardy, author of one of the grandest of realistic romances."

It is forgotten, however, how much wider is the fiction-reading public than of old; and probably the old-fashioned three-volume novel never had nearly so many devoted readers as now. The short story is after all nothing so very new; and a generation and more ago, Edgar Allen Poe showed what could be done in this direction, while in France the short story long since attained a singular degree of perfection. It is a fashion of the later nineteenth-century times to resuscitate old forms and then present them as new.

Among those who have decidedly made a mark with the short story are Mr. Barrie, Mr. Quiller Couch, Mrs. W. K. Clifford, author of *Love Letters of a Worldly Woman*, and Mr. Zangwill, one of our later novelists. Supreme probably among these and a few more are Mr. Robert Louis Stevenson and Rudyard Kipling, who first attracted notice in India by his *Departmental Ditties*. Then came his tales relative to military, native and social life in India; and did he not write, too, the *Light that*

Failed?   That Rudyard Kipling possesses genius
we will freely concede ; but it is one thing to have
genius and another to use it to the best ends.   To
some minds the prominence given to the vulgar
characteristics of the private soldier is no doubt
an offence, as it tends to induce a complacent
acquiescence in traits of character which we
would wish all who possess them to put off on the
first convenient opportunity.   There is room in
the great world of literature for all types of writers,
doubtless ; but those who generally confine themselves to the delineation of what is not exactly
heroic or elevating in humanity, are not likely to
communicate to their readers more than the
pleasure of the moment.   Well, that is, doubtless,
no small thing in days when everybody is clamour-
ing for more mental distraction, simply, perhaps,
because many people cannot endure their own
companionship,—a natural result of the inner
moral atmosphere created by the materialistic
force of the times.

Among other short stories or collections of stories
may be mentioned *Two Offenders*, by " Ouida ".   In
this work we have as motors, assassination and
ingratitude, and in one instance Miss Ramée certainly gives us a fine analysis of character.   Another collection of tales is entitled the *Way they
Lived at Grimpat*, by Mrs. E. Rentoul Esler, a new

novelist, I believe; while, as an excursion into the
regions of the terrible, is the *Temple of Death*, by
Edmund Mitchell; then there is *Steve Brown's
Bunyip* and other stories, by John Arthur Barry.

Although not exactly a novelist, some mention
is fitting of the late Mr. R. M. Ballantyne, who
achieved quite a supreme distinction, as a popular
writer of books of stirring adventure for boys.
Captain Marryat himself penned some capital
works for the young, such as *Masterman Ready*
and the *Little Savage;* but Ballantyne was equally
at home whether at sea or on land. His range
was world-wide, from Greenland to the Edens of
the South Seas; and through his agency, undoubtedly a vast amount of sound information as to
the manners and customs, beliefs and habits of
the various aborigines throughout Asia, Africa,
and America has been disseminated.

In regard to moral tales for the young, Elizabeth
Sewell must not be omitted. This prolific author
became known as a writer of High Church fiction
by her *Amy Herbert,* published as long ago as 1844.
This was followed by *Gertrude,* the *Earl's Daughter,
Laneton Parsonage,* and very many more.

CHAPTER XV

TEMPERANCE NOVELS.

THERE is a large and an increasing literature devoted to temperance, and it is pretty certain that
much solid and extending good has resulted thence.
Of late years this form of fiction with a purpose has
much increased. It may be said in some measure
to have begun as a literary power with Mrs. Henry
Wood's remarkable prize story *Danesbury House*, a
work, by the way, which was the real cause of this
popular novelist obtaining a hearing. Since then,
a host of books, many, it must be admitted, of small
value, have poured forth ; and among these are some
that undoubtedly possess special merit. One of
the latest is entitled *Victims to Custom*, by Emily
Foster ; and here we have in one Edgar Grantley,
at one and twenty, a type of many of the young
men of the day. "He was not altogether a
vicious young man, although he possessed those
vices, small vices they are often termed, common
to multitudes of young men of the present day, *viz.*,
he smoked and drank." Another type is Godfrey

Antrim, who exercises a malign influence on Harold York, a dissenting minister's son; and here we are shown how "a little drinking," among young men especially, may easily lead to serious evils, to gambling, and ultimately to ruin. A more lamentable example of the vice of intemperance is afforded in this temperance tale, in Cynthia, who has at last to enter "a home for inebriates," so terrible is her craving for alcohol; while numerous other characters are depicted as slaves to drink. We need not go so far back as Plato to learn that the drunkard is not profitable for any kind of good service, or to another moralist, who rightly reminds us that troops of Furies march in the drunkard's triumph. Certain it is that habitual intemperance is an appalling vice; but still I hold that while it is impossible to make the whole world teetotal, it is possible to make the whole world temperate, which is the rational mean; and there is room here for a powerful writer who should show us how much nobler it is, morally, to drink in unfailing moderation—for wine is certainly a divine gift—and thereby evince the restraining influence of a high moral tone, than to totally abstain from alcohol, which may be called the main force form of moral self-restraint; and it is really but one more illustration of the falsehood of extremes.

To revert for a moment to what we may justly

deem the initial temperance novel, Mrs. Wood's *Danesbury House*, it may be observed that its origin was somewhat notable. Over thirty years ago, the directors of the Scottish Temperance League offered a prize of £100 for the best temperance tale; and the arbitrators were unanimously in favour of *Danesbury House*, a story sent in by Mrs. Henry Wood, and prefiguring in a remarkable manner the special qualities which were to mark a long series of delightfully domestic novels, *East Lynne* being the particular book that confirmed the success of *Danesbury House*. The opening of this prize story is tragic. Mr. Danesbury, a rich manufacturer, nearly loses his little boy through the blundering of a drunken nurse, and his wife is actually killed through a drunken gatekeeper letting a gate swing back on her horses as she is driving home, and causing them to bolt. Miss St. George, a sister of Mr. Serle, a friend of Mrs. Danesbury, comes to take the place of the lost mother, and makes herself agreeable to everybody, having an obvious end in view. The children had been brought up as water drinkers by their mother; but Miss St. George persuades all but one to drink wine; and we see here the unsuspected but direct beginning of the end.

The working out of the story is effective. When

the second Mrs. Danesbury finds her nurse intoxi-
cated, the latter retorts that the mistress herself
drinks strong ale and spirits afterwards; and if to
do so is shameful for a hard-working servant, what
is it then for a mistress? The second Mrs. Danesbury brings up the children—all but two, who remain true to what they knew to be their dead
mother's desire—to drink strong drinks; and then
we have graphic scenes of low industrial life at the
" Pig and Whistle," a mixture of mirth and sad-
ness; for the sketches are most amusing, while at
the same time the suggestiveness is painful, and
some of the incidents are heartrending. As time
passes on, the second Mrs. Danesbury becomes
more and more injudicious and unreasonable. and·
very wicked; and horrible things eventually come
to pass, all through intemperance. The suicide of
one of the sons is really one of the most powerful
things in all Mrs. Wood's numerous novels; and
is wrought up with that art which moves us as
Nature itself. If *Danesbury House* is not quite
a great book, it misses being one by very little
indeed.

This class of literature is much on the increase,
and has already wrought great and enduring good.
Here, indeed, may be found additional evidence of
the power for moral good that is inherent in fiction
when rightly directed towards moral ends. Not

only, too, has the temperance novel effected much
in the way of influencing people towards sobriety,
but it has also exercised a wholesome influence on
fiction generally ; and we do not often find even the
most popular novelists of the day—writers avowedly
without purpose beyond that of amusing—introducing drunken orgies at once to sing pæans of
praise over the mighty men of two or three
bottles !

CHAPTER XVI

SOME LIVING NOVELISTS: BRITISH AND AMERICAN.

IN the case of living novelists, it is by no means easy to assign to them definite places in the literary Valhalla. Popularity is no true measure of literary quality; and then again, while a novelist still produces, how can we tell what surprise he may yet have for his readers? After middle age, the first Lord Lytton produced an entirely new kind of romance; and clearly, until a novelist has ceased to write, it is unfair to pronounce absolutely on his or her merits; and in point of fact from a literary view-point, it is only in a succeeding generation that the real value of any fiction can be properly ascertained, and not always so soon.

It will be found convenient to give here, in alphabetical order, brief notices of the principal living writers of British and American fiction. Some of these are necessarily mentioned or alluded to under other sections; but here are grouped for ready reference the principal living exponents of contemporary British fiction, who in their respective ways are more or less still amusing the great and growing world of novel-readers.

Taking female novelists first, we note the following :—

Mrs. Leith Adams has published several novels, which have attained so much popularity and public favour generally. Among her best works of fiction are probably *Aunt Hepsy's Foundling, Louis Draycott, Geoffrey Stirling* and *Bonnie Kate*.

Mrs. Alexander is the author of a good many novels which have won favour with many readers. Among her principal novels may be mentioned *A Woman's Heart, Blind Fate, By Woman's Wit, Mammon, Her Dearest Foe, Valeria's Fate, The Wooing O't*, and the *Executor*.

Miss Mary Anderson is a lady who has published a curious novel entitled *A Son of Noah*. This is a singular story about Shem principally, wherein great, and sometimes vivid, verisimilitude has been achieved. The "giants" of Scripture are introduced, and though much familiar to readers of the Old Testament is introduced, the work is devoid of any touch of irreverence. For one thing it gives a strongly drawn picture of the wickedness into which mankind had fallen, and affords a glimpse of what some of the descendants of Cain had come to. The story ends with a striking account of the Deluge.

Mrs. G. Linnæus Banks (1821), *née* Varley. Her first novel, *God's Providence House* (1865), established her reputation. Since, she has written the *Manchester Man*, *Glory*, *Wooers and Winners*, and some weird tales.

Mrs. A. E. Barr (1831), *née* Huddleston, an American novelist, has written numerous fictions. *Friend Oliver* appeared in the *Century*, 1890.

Miss Ada Bayly (1860), better known as "Edna Lyall". Her first story, *Won by Waiting*, appeared in 1879. One of her best known works is *A Hardy Norseman;* a large novel is *Doreen*.

Miss Matilda Betham-Edwards (1836). Her earliest story, the *White House by the Sea*, published when she was only nineteen, is popular still, and has been translated into Norse. Among her best known novels are *John and I*, *Doctor Jacob*, and *Kitty*.

Mrs. J. G. Bettany (1857) is the author of a successful novel of life in the Staffordshire black country entitled the *House of Rimmon*.

Mrs. E. M. Booth, better known as "Rita," has been a prolific novelist. Among her leading novels may be enumerated : *After Long Grief and Pain*, *Corinna*, *Dame Durden*, *Darby and Joan*, *My Lady Coquette*, *My Lord Conceit*, and *A Sinless Secret*.

Miss Braddon will be found sufficiently dealt with elsewhere. This prolific lady novelist has now written more than fifty three-volume novels, and appears as fertile in invention and as vivid in imagination as ever.

Miss Rhoda Broughton (1840) first made a mark with a novel called *Cometh up as a Flower*. Other of her typical novels are : *Not Wisely, but too Well, Red as a Rose is She*, and *Nancy*.

Mrs. Frances Burnett (1849), *née* Hodgson, was born at Manchester, but ultimately settled in the United States. One of her first successful novels was *That Lass o' Lowrie's ;* but it was her striking and in many respects touching story *Little Lord Fauntleroy* that first won for her real popularity.

Mrs. Mona Caird is mainly known by a novel called the *Wing of Azraël*, wherein are worked up some new and daring speculative notions on woman in connection with the marriage state.

Miss Ada Cambridge is the author of several novels ; of these may be mentioned *A Little Minx*, the *Three Miss Kings*, and *All in Vain*.

Mrs. H. Lovett Cameron is the author of some dozen or more novels, among which may be cited the *Cost of a Lie, Deceivers Ever, Pure Gold,* and *Worth Winning*.

Miss Rosa N. Carey is the writer of many popular novels. Among these may be mentioned the following : *Aunt Diana, Averil, For Lilias, Only the Governess, Queenie's Whim, Uncle Max, Wooed and Married*.

16

Mrs. Amélie Rives (1863) has attracted notice by her novel *Quick or the Dead*, issued 1888, and Mrs. E. Charles by her series *The Chronicles of the Schönberg-Cotta Family*.

Miss Mary Cholmondeley is the author of several successful three-volume novels, among which may be mentioned the *Danvers Jewels* and *Sir Charles Danvers*. A later novel by this lady is entitled *Diana Tempest*, wherein will be found a good deal of moral anatomy.

Miss Mabel Collins has produced several novels of much merit and interest. Notably one entitled the *Prettiest Woman in Warsaw*. A later novel, *Juliet's Lovers*, is decidedly vivacious.

Miss Marie Corelli must not be overlooked here, seeing that she has attracted much notice by her highly sensational novels, of which *Ardath, Vendetta*, and *Thelma* are types. A later work is *Barabbas*, a romance founded on the Gospels.

Mrs. Craigie, who writes under the pen-name of "John Oliver Hobbes," is a recent writer of fiction. One of her works is curiously called *A Bundle of Life*, and was published in December, 1893, in the Pseudonym library.

Mrs. Margaretta Wade Deland, *née* Campbell, was born at Alleghany, Pennsylvania, U.S.A., 1857, studied at Cooper Union, New York, and taught in the Girls' Normal College in the Empire City.

Her mark was made in fiction when in 1888 she published *John Ward, Preacher*, a novel which, at the time, attracted much notice. She is the writer of *Florida Days*, etc.

Mrs. A. M. Diehl is the author of the *Garden of Eden*, and *A Woman's Whim*.

Lady Dilke has published one work of fiction which has excited some interest, *viz.*, the *Shrine of Death*, 1886.

Miss Sarah Doudney (1842) is a most prolific story teller, and has long been recognised as a pure and popular novelist for girls.

Miss Amelia Edwards has produced many novels since she first attracted attention in 1864 with a novel called *Barbara's History*. Miss Edwards, by the way, is a great traveller, and an eminent Egyptologist.

Miss Annie Edwards is the author of several novels. Among those best known are *Archie Lovell, A Ballroom Repentance, Ought We to Visit Her ? Pearl Powder*, and *Susan Fielding*.

Miss Emily Faithfull (1835) is the author of one novel entitled *Change upon Change*. Miss Faithfull's work on behalf of her sex is well known.

Miss Jessie Fothergill ought not to be passed over unmentioned, seeing that she has produced some excellent novels. One of her notable works is *First Violin*.

Mrs. Sarah Grand is best known as the author of the *Heavenly Twins*, a novel that has excited an extraordinary amount of interest.

Miss Iza Duffus Hardy has written many novels, among which are *A New Othello, Love, Honour and Obey*, and *Only*—a love story.

Miss Beatrice Harraden has written several short stories, and made a mark with a rather striking novel entitled *Ships that pass in the Night*.

Mrs. Henniker has produced some fiction noticeable for its quality. Her latest volume is entitled *Outlines*, and includes four remarkably good stories, of which *A Statesman's Love Lapse* is clever.

Mrs. Cashel Hoey (1830) is mainly known as a novelist by her two novels, the *Lover's Creed* and *A Stern Chase*. Mrs. Alfred Hunt must be included.

Mrs. Houstoun is the writer of several well-known novels; among the principal are: *Recommended to Mercy, Barbara's Warning, A Heart of Fire*, and *His Besetting Sin*.

Mrs. Hungerford, *née* Miss Margaret Wolfe Hamilton, has won much popularity by her novel *Molly Bawn*, and has also published *Phyllis, A Born Coquette*, and other works of fiction, wherein there is a remarkable flow of natural dialogue, and much clever characterisation. Some remarks on Mrs. Hungerford's special characteristics as a writer of fiction occur in a previous chapter.

Mrs. Robert Jocelyn is the author of *Drawn Blank*, the *M. F. H.'s Daughter*. Her latest novel is entitled *Pamela's Honeymoon*.

Dr. Arabella Kenealy is a daughter of the famous Dr. Kenealy, who, as advocate for the claimant in the historic Tichborne trial, obtained a world-wide celebrity. Miss Kenealy is a lady of great intellectual attainments, and is distinguished in medical science. Of this she has given abundant evidence in her successful novel entitled *Dr. Janet of Harley Street*. The novel in question enters largely on the great Woman's Rights Question, and delineates the feelings of a young and sensitive girl who is forced into a loveless marriage with a rich man, old enough to be her father, and from whom on her wedding day she escapes. Casting herself on London, she tries to obtain employment as a hospital nurse, and thus comes in the way of the Dr. Janet of the story. Miss Kenealy has since published *Molly and Her Man-o'-War*, and *Some Men are Such Gentlemen*.

Miss Rosa Mackenzie Kettle is a rather prolific novelist. One of her latest works is *Rose, Shamrock, and Thistle*. Love-making forms the staple of the story, and the tone is pure throughout. A novel wherein none of the commandments is broken is rather refreshing amid the deluge of highly sensational fiction that now pours forth.

Mrs. E. Linton (1822) began her career in fiction with *Azeth the Egyptian,* and is the author of many stories, among which may be noticed the *World well Lost* and the *Rebel of the Family.* Miss Emily Lawless is another well-known novelist.

Mrs. K. S. Macquoid has produced some distinctive novels. Among these may be mentioned *A Bad Beginning, At an Old Chateau, Beside the River, Diane, Drifting Apart, Elinor Dryden, The Faithful Lover, Forgotten by the World, Joan Wentworth, Louisa, Patty,* and *Too Soon.* Mrs. Macquoid's latest novel is entitled *In an Orchard.*

Miss Florence Marryat (Mrs. Francis Lean), the sixth daughter of the famous Captain Marryat, commenced her career as a novelist in 1865 with *Love's Conflict.* One of her latest works is *There is no Death ;* another is entitled *The Beautiful Soul.*

Mrs. Herbert Martin is the author of *Bonnie Leslie,* etc., and of *Britomart,* which is concerned mainly with an example of noble womanhood.

Mrs. L. T. Meade has produced some charming tales, which may be termed in some cases novels suited for young readers. Among the most auspicious are *Daddy's Boy, A World of Girls,* and the *O'Donnels of Inchfawn.* Her later novels include *A Soldier of Fortune, The Medicine Lady, In an Iron Grip,* and *A Life for a Soul.*

Miss Jean Middlemass has put forth several novels which have obtained recognition. Among these are *Poisoned Arrows, A Girl in a Thousand,* and *Sealed by a Kiss.* A later work is the *Mystery of Clement Dunraven.*

Mrs. M. L. Molesworth (*née* Stewart), although greatly identified with tales for young girls, has written several novels, of which *Lover and Husband, Cicely,* and *Not Without Thorns,* are the most distinctive. Mrs. Molesworth is also the author of the *Palace in the Garden,* and many very pleasing tales for the young.

Mrs. Needell is the author of a novel, *Stephen Ellicott's Daughter,* which on its appearance won immediate recognition for its force and naturalness. Other of her novels are *Julian Karslake's Secret, Passing the Love of Women,* and *Philip Methuen.*

Mrs. Margaret Oliphant (1828) is one of the most prolific of lady novelists. Her novel *Caleb Field* appeared as long ago as 1850. Among her best known novels are the *Chronicles of Carlingford, Lady Carr, Sons and Daughters, Hester, Sir Tom, Madam, Lucy Crofton;* and an extraordinary study of the supernatural, entitled *A Beleaguered City.*

Mrs. Louisa Parr has in her novel *Dorothy Fox* (1870) given a pleasing glimpse of life among the Society of Friends; another novel of hers which has attracted notice is entitled *Adam and Eve.*

Miss Frances Mary Peard has published several novels, including the *Rose Garden*, *Near Neighbours*, *To Horse and Away*, etc.

Mrs. E. R. Pitman (1841) is the author of *Vestina's Martyrdom*, a story of the catacombs, *Profit and Loss*, and other novels of fiction.

Mrs. Campbell Mackworth Praed (1852) is an Australian born ; and her first novel, published in 1888, is entitled *An Australian Heroine ;* a later novel is called the *Romance of a Station*. Mrs. Praed has had long personal experience of life in the Queensland bush.

Mrs. Reeves, *née* Helen Mathers (1852), began her career as a novelist with *Comin' thro' the Rye*. Among her best known novels are *My Lady Green Sleeves*, the *Story of a Sin*, and *Found out*.

Mrs. Riddell, born in County Antrim, has written a number of fine novels, among which *George Geith*, *Too Much Alone*, *City and Suburb*, and the *Senior Partner*, are notable in their respective ways.

Mrs. R. Ritchie, daughter of the great novelist Thackeray, began her literary life with the *Story of Elizabeth* (1863), which was at once successful. One of her best known works is *Blue Beard's Key*.

Miss Roberts has issued some highly noteworthy novels and tales, whereof that entitled *Atelier du Lys* is decidedly distinctive. Among others may be noted : *A Child of the Revolution*, the *Fiddler of*

Lugan, Mademoiselle Mori, In the Olden Time, Hester's Venture, That Child, and *Under a Cloud.*

Miss Dora Russell is the author of numerous novels, among which *Footprints in the Snow* and *The Vicar's Governess* are notable. Her latest novels are entitled *A Hidden Chain, A Country Sweetheart,* and *The Other Bond.*

Miss Olive Schreiner is the daughter of a Lutheran clergyman in Cape Town. Her novel, the *Story of an African Farm,* attracted great notice by reason of its novelty. She is an advocate of loving-kindness as the greatest agency for good.

Mrs. Arthur Stannard (1856), known as " John Strange Winter," is, according to Mr. Ruskin, the author to whom we owe the most finished and faithful rendering ever given of the British soldier. Her story *Bootles' Baby* attracted universal attention as soon as it appeared. Among her novels are *Beautiful Jim, My Poor Dick, Mignon's Secret,* and many more.

Mrs. Harriet Elizabeth Stowe (1812) is the famous author of *Uncle Tom's Cabin,* 1852, which has been translated into over twenty languages. Mrs. Stowe has produced many other novels, of which the most noteworthy are the *Minister's Wooing, Dred, a Tale of the Dismal Swamp,* the *Pearl of Orr's Island,* and others. Mrs. Stowe and her genius are fully dealt with in the chapter devoted to "American Novels".

Miss Annie S. Swan has written a great number of novels and tales. The principal are : *Across her Path, Aldersyde, Briar and Palm, Gates of Eden, St. Veda's, Sheila,* and *Twice Tried.*

Miss Annie Thomas (Mrs. Pender Cudlip) has been a prolific producer of novels and tales, some of which have attained much popularity. Among these are : *On Guard, Walter Goring, Called to Account, Blotted Out, Kate Valliant, High Stakes, A Laggard in Love, Allerton Towers,* and *He cometh not, she said.* Her latest novel is *False Pretences.*

Miss Sarah Tytler has exhibited great fecundity in fiction. Among her best known novels and tales are : *Citoyenne Jacqueline, Noblesse Oblige, Buried Diamonds,* and *Beauty and the Beast.*

Mrs. Lucy B. Walford is the author of *Bee or Beatrix, Pauline, Cousins, Troublesome Daughters,* and numerous other novels. The *Mischief of Monica* is one of the latest.

Mrs. Herbert D. Ward, *née* Elizabeth Stuart Phelps (1844), is an American novelist, who began to write for the press at the age of only thirteen. Among her best known works are the *Gates Ajar, Burglars in Paradise, Men, Women, and Ghosts,* etc.

Mrs. Humphry Ward (1851) is a grand-daughter of the famous Dr. Arnold of Rugby. Her one great novel is *Robert Elsmere,* which in five months went through seven editions. I have dealt with this work fully under "Religious Novels". Mrs. Ward is the author also of *David Grieve*, and of *Marcella*, her latest novel.

Mrs. Hibbert Ware has written several novels, among which are *Fairfax of Fuyston*, *The King of Bath*, and *Friend Ellwood*.

Mrs. Adeline Whitney (1824) is an American author of fiction, chiefly for the young.

Mrs. Margaret Woods is the author of *A Village Tragedy*, *Esther Vanhomrigh*, and other novels.

Miss Charlotte Mary Yonge (1823) is the author of several fine novels, of which the *Heir of Redcliffe*, *Heartsease*, the *Daisy Chain*, and the *Lances of Lynwood* are the best known.

The lady who writes under the name of " Curtis Yorke " has produced several highly sensational novels and tales. The most noteworthy are *Hush*, *Once*, and *Dudley*.

We now turn to male novelists.

Mr. Grant Allen (1848) is a novelist who began first as a distinctly scientific writer, and was much identified with Darwinian ideas. In 1883, Mr. Allen began writing fiction, and has produced several well-known novels, *Philistia*, the *Devil's Die*, and the *Tents of Shem* being among the number.

Mr. Edwin Lester Arnold has produced some excellent novels and romances. One of these is

entitled the *Constable of St. Nicholas*, another is
the *Wonderful Adventures of Phra the Phœnician*.
This last calls up in a highly realistic way the
manners and customs of a race that has entirely
vanished, and which has left fewer traces behind
than, perhaps, any other people equally dominant in
their day.   .

Mr. J. M. Barrie (1860) is fully referred to under
" Comic and Humorous Novels ".

The Rev. Sabine Baring-Gould (1834) commenced his literary career in general literature,
and is well known for his erudite work the *Lives
of the Saints*. Subsequently he turned his attention to fiction, and wrote some highly successful
novels, among which are *Mehalah, John Herring,*
and *Court Royal.*

Mr. E. F. Benson has achieved great contemporary success through his novel entitled *Dodo: a
Detail of the Day*. The interest of the book appears
to pivot mainly on the presentation of certain social
phases in life; and moreover it is amusing. No
final judgment can properly be passed upon books
only recently before the world. It is, however, a
fact that *Dodo* ran to a thirteenth edition quite
early, and that few novels of the latter years of the
nineteenth century have been so successful. As
a two-volume novel it rapidly went through ten
editions, and one of the most critical reviews pro-

nounced it to be a perpetual feast of epigram and paradox, while undoubtedly it is a witty sketch of society. Mr. Benson has since produced a novel entitled *The Rubicon*.

Mr. Walter Besant (1838) practically commenced his career as a novelist when in 1871 he entered into a literary partnership with the late Mr. James Rice, and produced in collaboration several novels. Subsequently Mr. Besant produced by himself quite a series of fine fictions, of which *All Sorts and Conditions of Men, For Faith and Freedom,* and *All in a Garden Fair*, are much admired.

Mr. William Black (1841), originally a journalist, published his first novel, *Love or Marriage*, in 1867. This novel did not succeed, being occupied too much with social problems. Mr. Black's next novel, *In Silk Attire*, was successful ; and since has been followed by a number of novels, many of which have been very popular. Mr. William Black's latest three-volume novel, the *Handsome Humes*, is a curious story ; for the heroine is the daughter of an ex-pugilist, and the hero, by way of antithesis, is one whose pride of birth is intense. The scenes are laid in the beautiful country round Henley, and are coloured with Mr. Black's usual force when describing Nature.

Mr. Richard Blackmore (1825) is the author of *Lorna Doone*, a romance I have fully dealt with elsewhere.   Mr. Blackmore is the writer too of *Clara Vaughan*, *Alice Lorraine*, and other fine novels.

Mr. Robert Buchanan (1841) began as a poet; but in 1871 his first novel, the *Shadow of the Sword*, a powerful story of the Napoleonic régime, attracted much attention, and since then he has produced some striking novels.

Mr. George Cable (1844) is an American novelist, and has particularly distinguished himself by his great knowledge of the creole character as shown in his novels dealing with creole life, his principal works being *Madame Delphine*, the *Creoles of Louisiana*, and *Old Creole Days*.

Mr. Hall Caine as a novelist has won great distinction by his romance the *Deemster*, wherein he evinces a remarkable acquaintance with Manx manners; the *Scrapegoat* is another of his novels, and in the *Bondman* he gives very graphic pictures of Iceland and its people.   The *Manxman* is a later work which has been highly praised.

Mr. A. T. Quiller Couch, writing originally simply as " Q," is the author of many notable novels of an extremely romantic type.   The principal of these are *Blue Pavilions*, *Dead Man's Rock*, the *Splendid Spur*, and *Troy Town;* not forgetting *I saw Three Ships*.

Mr. Francis Marion Crawford (1854) has had much personal experience of life in India, as shown in his novel *Mr. Isaacs.* He is the author of several novels, such as *Zoroaster, A Cigarette Maker's Romance,* and *Marzio's Crucifixion.* Mr. Oswald Crawfurd also merits mention.

Mr. S. R. Crockett is the author of a curious story entitled the *Stickit Minister.* His later work is the *Raiders, or Some Passages in the Life of John Faa, Lord and Earl of Little Egypt.* The scene is laid here in the wild west of Scotland in olden days; in this Scotch romance we have delineations of Solway smugglers, and gipsies. Mr. Crockett's latest novel is a love story entitled *The Lilac Sunbonnet.*

Sir George Webb Dasent (1824) is a prolific writer in history and myths, especially in things Icelandic and Norse generally; but he has written some novels, among which are *Annals of an Eventful Life, Three to One,* and *Half a Life.*

Mr. Conan Doyle is fully dealt with under "Historical Novels"; but we must not pass over his very remarkable creation in sensational fiction —Sherlock Holmes—quite a new study in detectives, and involving a series of startling incidents, which caused this work to have a great vogue.

Mr E. Downey is another well-known novelist.

Mr. B. L. Farjeon commenced his career in fiction with *Grif,* which ran through many editions in England and America, and has long been recognised as a standard Australian novel. *Joshua Marvel* followed, and was pronounced one of the purest stories of the age. *Blade o' Grass* succeeded, and its phenomenal success revived interest in Christmas numbers, so that for many years Mr. Farjeon's Christmas fictions were extremely popular. Subsequent stories are *Bread and Cheese and Kisses*, *Golden Grain*, the *King of Noland*, and *Shadows on the Snow*. The first editions of these were, it is said, never less than 25,000 copies. Mr. Farjeon produced later what many critics pronounce his finest work, *In a Silver Sea*, a piece of pure idealism worked out in a story of human passion. Being urged to produce a sensational novel, his initial work of that kind, *Great Porter Square*, proved a marked success, and was followed by the *House of White Shadows*, the *Sacred Nugget*, *Devlin the Barber*, the *Nine of Hearts*, and others. Mr. Farjeon's book for children, the *Golden Land*, is very popular; and a tale of fancy and humour, entitled *Something Occurred*, issued in 1893, was eagerly welcomed. Mr. Farjeon's fictions have been translated into German, French, Italian, and Spanish, etc. In reference to *Great Porter Square* the *Athenæum* declared Mr. Farjeon to be "one of the best of a long line of story-tellers, descended through Wilkie Collins from Defoe".

Mr. George Manville Fenn (1830) began his career in fiction as a writer of tales for boys, but subsequently he developed into a novelist; and some of his novels, notably *Eli's Children*, relative to the wild sons of a country clergyman, are marked by much force and a vivid imagination.

Mr. Percy H. Fitzgerald (1834) has produced much in general literature, but he has also written several novels, among which are *Bella Donna, Diana Gay,* and the *Lady of Brantome.*

Mr. R. E. Francillon (1841) is a general writer; but as a novelist he is the author of *Earl's Dene, Pearl and Emerald,* and *Strange Waters,* etc.

Mr. Harold Frederic is the author of several novels. Among these may be mentioned the *Return of the O'Mahony, In the Valley,* and the *Copperhead.*

Mr. Ernest Glanville is the author of several interesting novels, among which may be cited the *Lost Heiress,* and *A Fair Colonist.*

Mr. Henry Rider Haggard (1856) was in the first Zulu War a lieutenant of the Pretoria horse, and there acquired much information on things African. In 1884 he issued a novel called *Dawn,* and another entitled the *Witch's Head,* and two years later in his romance of *King Solomon's Mines* produced a work that became at once popular. Then came *She,* and several other highly sensa-

17

tional novels. I have referred to *She* in another
place. A later romance by Mr. Haggard is *Monte-
zuma's Daughter*.

Mr. George Halse is more properly a sculptor ;
but he has written several novels, among which
are *Weeping Ferry* and *Phil Hathaway's Failures*.

Mr. Thomas Hardy (1840) was at first an
architect ; and in his earliest novel, *Desperate Re-
medies*, this fact is very apparent. One of Mr.
Hardy's best known novels is probably *Far from
the Madding Crowd*. Others of his novels are the
Trumpet Major, *Two on a Tower*, the *Woodlanders*,
Tess of the D'Urbervilles, a true woman faithfully presented. Mr. Hardy revels in rustic
dialect, and in descriptions of Southern England.

Mr. Francis Bret Harte (1839) is an American
humorist and poet, but he is the author of several
novels, among which may be mentioned *Maruja*
and *A Ward of the Golden Gate*.

Mr. Joseph Hatton (1839) commenced his literary career as a journalist, but is now known as a
novelist. *Clytie*, *Cruel London*, and the *Queen of
Bohemia*, are among his principal novels. *By
Order of the Czar*, a later romance, has been prohibited in Russia by reason of its fearless ex-
posure of the cruel treatment of the Jews in
Russia.

Mr. Julian Hawthorne (1846) is a son of the

eminent American novelist, Nathaniel Hawthorne, and much of his fiction is highly sensational. Among his novels are *Fortune's Fool* and *Dust*.

Mr. Joseph Hocking has produced several novels of a religious character. Among these are the *Monk of Mar-Saba*, and *Jabez Easterbrook*. Another distinctive work of Mr. Hocking's is *Elrad the Hic, a Romance of the Sea of Galilee*.

Mr. Anthony Hope is best known as the author of *Sport Royal, A Man of Mark, The Prisoner of Zenda*, and the *God in the Car*.

Mr. Tighe Hopkins (1856) has published several novels; *'Twixt Love and Duty* and *For Freedom* are among the number. In his later work, the *Nugents of Carriconna*, there are some capital vignettes of Irish peasants.

Mr. William Dean Howells (1837) is an American writer, and has published much excellent verse. He is the author of several good novels.

Mr. Henry James (1843) is the author of a good many novels, wherein the American appears as he is seen when travelling in Europe. Mr. James depends on his characterisation rather than on incident. The *Princess Casamassima* is one of his distinctive fictions.

Mr. C. F. Keary is the author of a realistic novel, entitled the *Two Lancrofts*, a fiction professing to delineate some of the worst phases of

English art student life in Paris. Another novel
by Mr. Keary is *Un Mariage de Convénance*.

Mr. Leslie Keith is a novelist of promise. His
recent novel in three volumes, *Lisbeth*, is somewhat unique. The initial chapters are concerned
with the members of a typical middle-class Scottish family, domiciled in the metropolis, but still
looking fondly back to their beloved birthplace,
and full of a race prejudice, which, however narrow and, perhaps, unreasonable, still excites a
certain sympathy in the reader. Mr. Keith is
very realistic.

Mr. Coulson Kernahan has only lately come
into notice as a fictionist, through the publication
of a singular work, entitled *A Dead Man's Diary*,
followed by *A Book of Strange Sins*.

Mr. Rudyard Kipling (1864) is the son of the
headmaster of the Lahore School of Art. He first
became prominent by *Plain Tales*, *The Gadsbys*, and
other highly original productions. His story, the
Light that Failed, attracted great notice on its first
appearance. He is remarkable for his intimate
acquaintance with military life in India at the
present day. A reference should be made here to
the late Mr. Wolcott Balestier, who collaborated
with Mr. Kipling in the *Naulakha*, and was himself
the author of the *Average Woman*, and of a posthumous novel entitled *Benefits Forgot*.

Mr. Justin McCarthy (1830) was originally a journalist, but has written several popular novels, among which are *A Fair Saxon, Donna Quixote,* and *Miss Misanthrope.*

Dr. George Macdonald (1824) is a poet as well as a novelist. The *Seaboard Parish, Robert Falconer,* and *Alec Forbes of Howglen,* are well known among his many fine novels. Mrs. Ian Maclaren must be cited too, as the author of *Beside the Bonnie Briar Bush.*

Mr. William Hurrell Mallock (1849), after writing much on sociology, published in 1886 a novel which has attracted much attention, under the title of the *Old Order Changes.*

Mr. George Meredith (1828) is a poet and a mystic first, and afterwards a novelist. His earliest novel to attract attention was *Rhoda Fleming,* while among his more distinctive novels are the *Adventures of Harry Richmond, The Egoist,* and *Diana of the Crossways.* Later novels are entitled *One of Our Conquerors* and *Lord Ormont and his Amnita.* Mr. Meredith's genius is fully dealt with in a previous section of this work.

Mr. Frank F. Moore is one of our most recent novelists, and is at present, perhaps, best known by his quaintly entitled novel *A Gray Eye or So.*

Mr. George Moore is a novelist of much force and eccentricity. He first attracted attention by his novel entitled *A Mummer's Wife*, and has since produced much realistic fiction of a peculiar type.

Mr. David Christie Murray was at first a journalist, but in 1879 he made a mark with his novel *A Life's Atonement*. Mr. Murray has indeed published a great number of novels and tales. The principal are: *Cynic Fortune, First Person Singular, Hearts, Joseph's Coat, Rainbow Gold,* the *Bishop's Bible, Wild Darril, John Vale's Guardian, Paul Jones alias,* and many others.

Mr. W. E. Norris is a novelist whose fiction has of late slowly but surely won a place of its own. Among the principal novels of Mr. Norris may be cited: *Chris, Heaps of Money, Mademoiselle de Mersac, Matrimony, The Rogue, Marcia,* and *Thirlby Hall.*

Mr. James Payn (1830) is as prolific a novelist as Miss Braddon. One of his most remarkable sensational novels is *By Proxy*, a tale of China, containing some thrilling situations. The *Heir of all the Ages,* and *A Prince of the Blood,* are among his later novels.

Mr. F. W. Robinson merits special notice on several accounts. He is the author of full fifty novels; and besides this enormous mass of fiction he published, under the *nom-de-plume* of the " Prison Matron," a series of volumes of interest and value on prison life. No one except Dickens has delineated so graphically low social types of ordinary life. His first great success was *Grandmother's Money;* but *High Church, No Church, Only a Waif, Mattie, a Stray,* and *Poor Humanity,* are remarkable fictions. I know no novelist who more realistically draws out true human interest from sordid pecuniary trials ; and his realism, exact as that of Zola, is always devoid of offence of any kind. Special interest attaches to the fact that it was Mr. Robinson who in a sense "discovered" the peculiar genius of Mr. Jerome K. Jerome by accepting the *Idle Thoughts of an Idle Fellow,* for his magazine *Home Chimes ;* and with Mr. Frederick Greenwood and Mr. Robertson Nicoll he also helped forward Mr. J. M. Barrie.

Mr. George R. Sims has, after much success as a journalist, a writer of homely ballads, and of stirring melodrama, produced some fiction. His principal novels are *Rogues and Vagabonds, The Ring o' Bells, Memoirs of Mary Jane, Mary Jane Married, Tales of To-day,* and *My Two Wives.*

The late Mr. R. L. Stevenson (1850-1894), author of *Treasure Island,* will be found dealt with under "Occult Novels". His latest work is entitled *The Ebb Tide,* produced in collaboration with Mr. Lloyd Osbourne.

Mr. Fallett Synge has written some noteworthy fiction.

Mr. H. B. Marriott Watson (1863) is the author of *Marahuna*, a romance of the antarctic circle, and of *Lady Faint Heart*. In 1891 he published the *Web of the Spider*, a tale of the Maori war in New Zealand, a very vivid work of great excellence; and in the same year Mr. Watson produced a play, entitled *Richard Savage*, in collaboration with Mr. J. H. Barrie.

Mr. W. Westall has produced a cluster of novels, among which are *Two Pinches of Snuff*, *Nigel Fortescue*, and *A Phantom City*.

Mr. Edmund Yates[1] (1831), in the Post Office originally like Anthony Trollope, has published a number of novels, of which *Broken to Harness*, *Black Sheep* and *Wrecked in Port*, are good types.

Mr. I. Zangwill is the author of some fiction which has been described as grotesque and fantastic, or, at all events, out of the common track. Mr. Zangwill won much popularity with his work entitled the *Children of the Ghetto;* and in a later effort, entitled the *King of Schnorrers*, we have much that is interesting relative to the manners and customs of the Jews as they were in London over a century ago.

---

[1] Mr. Yates died while this work was going through the press, on 19th May, 1894.

Chapter XVII.

AUSTRALIAN NOVELS.

It is only, comparatively speaking, of late years that it has been discovered that the Austral world has a species of fiction peculiar to itself. At his best, the novelist in his most Protean forms is but the universal prose poet ; and it is no way singular that the Australian poetry should have preceded Australian fiction, which, though still in its infancy, is full of vigorous promise for the future.

It is an arrestive fact to remember that under the Southern Cross no Australian ever gazes on a building more, or much more, than a century old ; and yet, although thus wanting in historic associative charm, Australia has undoubtedly much in its natural features which will, in due course, furnish to its writers inspiration as true as that which American writers have derived from their own backwoods, lakes, and prairies.

Australasia has a fauna and flora of its own. Just listen for a moment to one of Australia's own singers on the subject :—

> The eucalyptus blooms are sweet
> With honey; and the birds all day
> Sip the clear juices forth; brown, grey,
> A bird-like thing with tiny feet
> Cleaves to the boughs, or with small wings
> Amid the leafy spaces springs,
> And in the moonshine with shrill cries
> Flies bat-like where the white gums rise.

Thus sings an Australian poet of the flying mouse of New South Wales. Then we have the bell bird, whose song flows in

> Soft aerial chimes, unknown
> Save 'mid these silences alone;

while the flame trees of New South Wales and many other remarkable natural products all tend to give the Austral world a still life and a landscape distinctively its own.

At present Australian novelists are comparatively few; and, what is curious, unlike the early American fictionists, they are not generally remarkable for their word painting of the original natural features of the Austral world. One of the greatest, perhaps, of Australian novelists is Marcus Clarke, who emigrated to Victoria when a youth, and saw the very early and rough days before Australia had become really civilised. His one distinctive novel is entitled *For His Natural Life*, and, as may be imagined, relates to the convict times. It is a stirring piece of realism, and contains some terrible and but too vivid pictures of the cruelties of the authorities, and the atrocities of the convicts in the bad old times of transportation beyond the seas. A less known work of Marcus Clarke is entitled '*Twixt Shadow and Shine*.

Mr. B. L. Farjeon, who now resides in London, belongs to much more recent days. He began his literary career in New Zealand as a journalist, and soon drifted into fiction. He is the author of many charming novels, including *Joshua Marvel, Grif, A Young Girl's Life*, and many others, not forgetting his strong sensational story entitled *Richard Pardon's Peril*. In Mr. Farjeon's best work there is a vein of real poetry, and he has, moreover, a special faculty for the happy delineation of child life. *A Young Girl's Life* is rather a typical book of his. The main conception is simple enough. Evelina Durham is an orphan left to guardians, one of whom, being wholly unprincipled, consigns the child to the care of an aunt named Parker, who treats her with the most ingenious cruelty. Evelina is a bright lovable child, full of imagination; very touching, and at the same time charming, are the passages of the book where she is represented as imagining the butterflies, birds and flowers, to be connecting sympathising links between herself and her beloved parents, whom she refuses to regard as being buried at all! The wicked guardian seeks to force his ward to marry him, and thence arises a terrible struggle; for Evelina has formed a firm attachment for the hero of the story, in all ways worthy of her affections. Humour and fun abound in the persons of a ventriloquist, and a poetic butcher boy; but the charm of the book is in the delineation of the growth of Evelina's character.

As an Australian novelist in a certain sense, we must not overlook Henry Kingsley, brother of the famous author of *Hypatia,* who resided in Australia for six years, and produced as a result the *Hillyars and Burtons, Geoffry Hamlyn* and *Ravenshoe.* In the former will be found a graphic description of drought and of flood—those two great plagues of the Austral settler.

Many stirring stories have already appeared of the rough early days of Australian settlement, like Mr. Boldrewood's *Robbery under Arms,* and *Settlers and Convicts,* by Alexander Harris, which relate to the lawless side of life under the Southern Cross. As an example of the sensational is the novel entitled the *Mystery of a Hansom Cab,* which attained to an enormous circulation. This work, which is by Mr. W. Fergus Hume, has since been followed, however, by several much better fictions. Here, indeed, we touch a lower plane of literary work; for stories of this class owe their popularity to the crimes which they duly blazon forth in the most melodramatic manner, rather than to any true literary qualities. One of Mr. Fergus Hume's later strange romances is the *Harlequin Opal*. This is a medley of love, war, and wild adventure. The scene of the opening is in a Central American Republic, where a plot is in progress to overthrow the existing government. Four fast friends arrive, and then the adventures begin in earnest. Two of them are in love with two Spanish girls. The enormous opal, which is reverenced by the native with a kind of half worship, plays a great part in the narrative.

A writer of a different character is Mr. E. W. Hornung, who has quite recently struck out a new line in Austral fiction. His first success was achieved by a novel entitled *A Bride from the Bush*. In this tale the "bride" is a young Australian lady, who, being brought to England and introduced to her husband's family, becomes painfully aware of her social deficiencies. In a later novel entitled *Tiny Luttrell* we find again a young Australian lady as heroine; and her character has been drawn with its inconsistencies and contradictions finely discriminated.

Anno Domini 2000, or Woman's Destiny, by Sir Julius Vogel, must not be overlooked. The prologue is dated 1920, and is concerned with the

early trials of George Claude Sonsius, who falls a
martyr to poverty, and is made the means of opening up the first avenues to a gigantic social revolution.   The work really begins in A.D. 2000, and
starts in Melbourne, where the King of England
and Emperor of India is living in a fine palace on
the banks of the Yarra. The heroine, Hilda, is then
introduced, and an enormous amount of practical
politics and of socialist theories is ingeniously
interwoven into the texture of a very interesting
story.   At the close Sir Julius states that he has
sought to show that a recognised dominance of
either sex is unnecessary, and that men and
women may take part in the affairs of the world
on terms of equality.   Another object is to suggest
that the materials are to hand for forming the
dominion of Great Britain into a powerful and
beneficent empire; and finally the writer has a
strong conviction that every human being is entitled to a sufficiency of food and clothing, and to
decent lodging, whether or not he or she is willing to, or capable of, work.

One of the latest recruits to the ranks of Australian novelists is Mrs. A. Blitz.   Her first effort
was a three-volume novel entitled *An Australian
Millionaire*.   The plot is marked with much ingenuity; and the main action turns on an enormous
fortune, the heir to which is a changeling, and

seemingly not the lawful inheritor of almost un-
limited wealth.

Allusion should be made to a volume entitled *In
Australian Wilds*, a collection of colonial tales, by
C. Haddon Chambers, B. J. Farjeon, "Tasma";
and to *Oak Bough and Wattle Blossoms*, a series of
tales and sketches put forth by Mrs. Campbell
Praed, C. Haddon Chambers, Douglas B. W.
Sladen, E. S. Rawson, S. Oldmixon, and A. Patchett
Martin.

Mrs. Patchett Martin, the wife of the above,
is the writer of *Under the Gum Tree*, Australian
bush stories; and of a volume entitled *Coo-ee*,
being tales of Australian life by Australian
ladies.

Mrs. Campbell Mackworth Praed, *née* Rosa
Murray Prior, is a genuine Australian novelist.
This lady was born in Queensland, in 1852; and
her father, a leading Australian squatter, held
some high offices in more than one Queensland
Ministry. The subject of this sketch married a
nephew of the poet Praed, and for some years
lived on an island off the Queensland coast, and
thus had undoubtedly a romance-suggestive environment. Her initial novel, *An Australian Heroine*, was published in 1880, and was succeeded by
a number of distinctive fictions. One of her later
novels is *Outlaw and Lawmaker*.

Then there is Kenneth Mackay, who has de-lineated certain episodes and characteristics of Australian life with much picturesqueness and force. He has written in particular *Stirrup Jingles* and *Out Back*, the latter being a romance of the bush.

Mention may be made of *An Australian Girl*, by Mrs. Alick Macleod, which has attained the honour of a third edition.

One of the latest Australian novelists is Mr. Marriott Watson, of New Zealand, who first at-tracted attention by his remarkable romance, *Mara-huna*, wherein an imaginary expedition to discover the South Pole is made the agency of a very sen-sational story. Mr. Marriott Watson has since published a stirring story of the Maori struggle with the British power, under the title of *In the Spider's Web*.

Mr. Hume Nisbet is an Australian writer of fiction, who delineates vividly the scenery of the Austral world, and revels in scenes of adventure and peril. He is the author of *Ashes, Bail Up, A Bush Girl's Romance*, and several other stories of Austral life and scenery.

It is not very easy as yet to gauge the tastes of antipodean readers in respect to novels. The Librarian of the Free Public Library, Melbourne, Victoria, reported, less than two years after the opening of a lending department, that in eighteen months 130,000 works were taken out. I do not attach great value to Public Library statistics as indicating the intellectual and moral character of the community whereto they belong; but, of course, they have all the same value. It seems that the standard novelists are much read. "George Eliot" comes first, and Dickens is a long way behind Jules Verne and Mark Twain! A steady run is reported on the novels of Messrs. Besant, Black, Hardy, and Blackmore. Mr. George Meredith is reported as having but a small following. Finally, we learn that of the total issue of books 60 per cent. is composed of novels.

One of the very latest of Australian novels is entitled *Dave's Sweetheart*, by Mary Gaunt. This production in two volumes has more style than many of our antipodean fictionists possess. The author is stated to be an Australian who has never yet left her native soil, and the local colouring and general conception of the story is essentially Austral. The heroine Jenny will be new to most English readers, seeing that she is described as living in a police camp; and the working out of her character, that of Dave, and of the stepmother, who plays a salient part in the drama, is certainly highly effective.

18

In closing I should refer to Mrs. C. L. Waring Calvert, better known as Miss Atkinson, a native of New South Wales, who wrote *Gertrude, Cowanda, Hillicker* and other Australian tales. Madame Couvreur, too (Tasma), is a well-known Australian writer, her novel *Uncle Piper of Piper's Hill* having been a great success. Her second novel *In Her Earliest Youth* is likewise Australian. George Gordon M'Crae is well known on the Australian press and contributed a naval novel *Afloat and Ashore. or the Story of Oginski*, to the *Sydney Mail*. Miss Catherine Helen Spence, who has contributed many articles to the Austral press, has produced several novels, among which are *Clare Morrison*, a tale of the South Australian gold fever, *Tender and True, Mr. Hogarth's Will*, and *Gathered In*. Mrs. Ada Cross has written several novels, one being entitled *Up the Murray*. Mr. Gilbert Parker, who has attracted much attention by his fiction, is one of several Canadian novelists of marked merit.

No doubt Austral fiction will develop rapidly with the increase in the population of the principal colonies, and especially with the application of a very high average of national education to the whole people.

CHAPTER XVIII

AMERICAN NOVELS.

PROBABLY America is more truly distinctive in novelists than in poets. Poe forms, perhaps, the great exception; and he was, after all, a writer essentially of the sensational novel in its briefest forms as to quantity, but in its intensest phases as to force and quality. The fountain head of Transatlantic fiction is to be found in—

Charles Brockden Brown, who, born as long back as 1771, about a century ago published *Wieland*, which was succeeded by *Ormund, or the Secret Witness*, and subsequently by *Edgar Huntly, or the Adventures of a Sleep-Walker*, which probably suggested to the English novelist Henry Cockton the *Somnambulist*, a far inferior work. Brown was an ingenious, imaginative and psychological writer, and he invents incidents and analyses human nature in a masterly manner. Certainly he is often conspicuous for his departure from the realities of life, but for all that he is a very powerful and fascinating novelist.

James Fenimore Cooper I have already alluded to in connection with the fiction of the sea, but he was also a writer of novels relating to history and domestic life.   In his special series known as the " Leather-Stocking Tales," he has preserved for us enduring and strongly-coloured vignettes of the red men as they were in the early days of the North American settlement, when the back-woods were yet within a few days' journey of the Atlantic seaboard.   One series of novels gives us the life of the typical American backwoodsman at his very best—a worthy progenitor of the rail-splitting President to come.

In some respects the five novels composing the Leather-Stocking Series are unique and epochal in fiction.   Through them all runs the life-course of a man who is the best type of the American backwoodsman, and now represents an extinct race. In the *Deerslayer*, he first appears in his lusty youth, but quiet, modest, brave, and truthful; and in the charming episode of the Hutter family, living on a fortified floating ark on a lonely lake in the midst of hostile Indians, we have the tender delineation of the one attachment of the young backwoodsman, an attachment which endures with his life.   In his next stage of development, he is the *Pathfinder*, employed as a guide, and involved in the numerous conflicts of the day, when, to the disgrace of Europe, scalping red men were allowed to fight in line with regular troops. The third novel presents the Pathfinder in the prime of his physical power, as Hawkeye with his unerring rifle, and is called the *Last of the Mohicans.* Here we have French against English, and many thrilling episodes of Indian warfare, while a thread of romance is furnished by the sisters Alice and Cora, who, as the daughters of an officer on active service, are confided to the escort of Hawkeye and his companion, to guard them safely through a dangerous country, in order to join their father. Next comes the novel entitled the *Pioneers,* wherein Hawkeye, somewhat decayed in strength, is seen in rustic retirement, full of profound woodlore, and of sterling virtues ; and finally in the *Prairie,* we follow the veteran in his old age westward out of the backwoods, which have practically ceased to exist, until he finds, after further striking adventures, an euthanasia, from extreme old age, in the presence of that Nature which had ever been the one passion of his soul. Nowhere else in fiction is there quite a parallel to this fine and noble conception of an American woodman. Placed beside the roaring and boastful heroes of a later day, he is as Don Quixote beside a blatant bravo of Venice in the days of the Secret Ten. Courage, modesty, truth, honesty, and charity, are

personified in this one man, whose character was sufficient of itself to vitalise five whole novels; and had
Cooper written nothing else, this one delineation had
alone sufficed to ensure for him literary immortality.

Cooper wrote other Indian novels, one of the
most notable being the *Borderers*. This relates to
a New England settlement in the early Puritan
time, including among many thrilling incidents
the siege of a strong timber house by a number of
hostile Indians, who finally carry the building by
storm, when one of the settlers alone, holding a
strangled Indian before him in a narrow passage,
affords time for the women and children to take
refuge in a kind of keep, constructed in the midst
of the homestead, an incident probably founded
on some fact, or at all events tradition.

The *Bee Hunter* is another interesting novel. It
is laid in the Western forest, and teaches much of
natural history and of American woodcraft. One
of the characters ingeniously deceives some Indians
by broaching a puncheon of "firewater" into the
upper portion of a small river, and then persuades
the poor confiding savages that he is a mighty
"medicine man," who can change the rivers, if
so he pleases, into ardent spirits! In this story,
too, occurs one of Cooper's special delineations—
an old corporal who believes in the "bayonet" as
the only weapon to employ against the redskins.

Cooper was very versatile indeed; and in his *Spy*, by some pronounced his best novel, he deals with the great Revolution; and in Harvey Birch, a pedlar, depicts a concealed patriot, who, to serve his country, pretends to be a traitor! Much of the tale is finely wrought, and the end is extremely pathetic. *Lionel Lincoln* is mainly concerned with Bunker's Hill fight.

These novels, however, do not exhaust the long list of Cooper's fictions. He produced besides several historical novels dealing with interesting phases of European history. The *Bravo* relates to Venice in its days of power; and in *Mercedes* we have a phase of Spanish history in the days of Isabella and Ferdinand. Cooper has been somewhat neglected of late years. He was once extravagantly over-praised; but, making due allowance for all defects, he is unquestionably a great novelist, and if not the greatest that America has yet produced, he is still prominent among Transatlantic writers of fiction.

It is worth recording that in January, 1894, the grandniece of Cooper, Miss Constance Fenimore Woolson, while seriously ill at Florence, committed suicide under a sudden lapse of reason. Miss Woolson "inherited" some of her granduncle's genius, and was already a writer of promise.

Before passing on to America's greatest novelist

from some view-points, *viz.*, Nathaniel Hawthorne,
I would remark that American history has been
very amply dealt with by British novelists, where-
by I include here some of Transatlantic birth.
The fifteenth century is illustrated by Mr. R. M.
Ballantyne's the *Norsemen of the West*, dealing
with America before Columbus. The sixteenth
century is illustrated as to the early settlement in
Virginia by Mr. J. Powis in the *First Settlers in
Virginia*. The seventeenth century gives us the
First Settlers in New England by L. M. Child,
Pocahontas, by M. W. Moseby, and the *Narragansett
Chief, Pierce;* while the early settlement in Penn-
sylvania is set forth in *A True Hero*, by W. H. G.
Kingston. The eighteenth century naturally
yields a rich crop of novels. We have the old
French War in *Brandon*, O. Tiffany; the War for
Independence in *Mustang Grey*, Mark Twain (S. L.
Clemens); the *Five Stars of Texas*, J. W. Dallam;
the *White Scalper*, Aimard; and in a cluster of
novels by W. G. Sims. The dreadful struggle
between North and South has been illustrated by
J. E. Cooke in *Hilt to Hilt, Surrey of Eagle's Nest,
Mohun*, and in the *Confederate Spy* by J. H.
Crogie; while J. T. Trowbridge deals with the
same theme in *Cudjo's Cave*, the *Three Scouts*, and
the *Drummer Boy*. I have in the former portion
of this brief outline omitted Cooper's historic

romances, as they are referred to previously; and it must be confessed that in all the mass of literature that has appeared on American history, nothing has yet been put forth that is really commanding, or perhaps quite on a level with such a work even as Cooper's *Spy*, which deals so vividly and dramatically with the War of Independence.

We now pass to Nathaniel Hawthorne, who was born as long ago as 1804, and in a manner drifted into authorship. It was not until 1837 that a volume of his collected short fictions, contributed to various journals, appeared under the title of *Twice Told Tales*. Progress in his case was slow, for it was not until 1851 that a second volume was published; but meanwhile he had completed his *Mosses from an Old Manse*. The turning-point was reached in 1851 when the publication of the *Scarlet Letter* at once stamped him as a master in fiction, and the *House of the Seven Gables* was put forth the same year. Hawthorne was now recognised, not only by the discerning in America, but by European critics and people of culture, as an author richly endowed with poetic gifts, a fine imagination, and a fascinating style. Moreover, his fiction plainly displayed that he possessed a true instinctive insight into the depths of human nature, while with his obvious wealth of imagination was mingled a delicate humour. In 1852 he published the *Blithedale Romance*, which is usually regarded as a species of autobiography, being based to a certain extent on passages in his own life. He was now justly famous, and his friend President Pierce appointed him Consul at Liverpool. But his health had begun to fail, and after four years of official duty, he went to Italy to recruit his physical energies. This journey into classic lands furnished him with material and suggestions for a romance called *Transformation*. This is, with high imaginative merits, a fantastic fiction, although some of his admirers have pronounced it the best of his romances. He died in 1864, and after his death was published a work he had completed, entitled *Septimius, a Romance of Immortality*. Hawthorne is, perhaps, the most truly creative of American novelists, and some passages in the *Scarlet Letter*, and other of his fiction, belong to the higher planes of art.

Hawthorne's son — Julian Hawthorne — has written several novels, of which *Fortune's Fool* and *Dust* are the best examples, although in some of his later works he has evinced a tendency towards the more or less pronounced forms of sensationalism. Thus, for example, in his *Great Bank Robbery* he daringly depicts for heroine a young American beauty, blighted as to her affections in her first attachment, and determined to console herself with ambition as a substitute for love. She deceives her husband, a big genial clever man, named Nelson, we are told, with brains and a heart like a child. Mrs. Nelson has a passion for diamonds; and getting entangled with a man who deals in precious stones, she reveals to him for certain considerations the internal arrangements of the Manhattan Bank, wherewith she was familiar. Mrs. Nelson desires to be a leader of New York society, and in her downward course sticks at nothing. It is explained that her secret delight was to be at once a queen of New York fashion and an empress among thieves, aiding in colossal financial crimes that should convulse society! The story is told with power and some pathos. Grady, the diamond dealer, strives to become a better man; but this strange woman declares that she likes what is wrong, and breaks out in one scene with: "I'll tell you what I am. Did you ever see a water lily? They are the whitest flowers like me, and they grow in stagnant waters, out of the filthiest mud!" When Grady responds, saying that he is the old bull frog, croaking out at her, we are told that this delighted her much.

Another notable American contemporary novelist is Mr. Charles Henry Beckett, the author of

Who is John Noman? Here the reader is arrested by the opening description of the wonder of the good folk of Hickoryville, who one day saw the arrival of a stranger who was understood to have bought some miles of rock and cliffs, and worthless mountain land. He builds himself a strange house on the shoulder of Hickory mountain, and is soon known as the Master of the Mountains. In his solitary rambles he meets a strange rude boy, who had run away from ill usage, and, after giving the lad some milk, he thus addresses him : " My boy, you came whence you know not ; so do all mortals. Whither you and I go, we know not ; like all mortals. Why and whence ? Let us make common cause of our calamities. From this time forth you are John Noman,—that shall be your name." The strange recluse takes the boy to his house, which, although externally of rough timber and stone, is within tapestried in silk and gold, and adorned with costly Venetian mirrors. The Master of the Mountains educates John Noman, and prepares him for college, and then dies, leaving a will in favour of John. There is, of course, a mystery about the old recluse, and the story has an arch villain in an Italian named Gallori. There is a clique of dynamite anarchists for John to encounter ; and in the heroine we have a maiden as mysterious as the Master of the Mountains.

But to proceed : in Harriet Beecher Stowe we have a literary phenomenon, rather than an absolute literary genius ; although it may be objected that it was genius simply to see the opening that was offered for a novel treating of slavery just at the happy time, and to fill that opening so completely with *Uncle Tom's Cabin*. Let it not be supposed that I in any way desire to detract from Mrs. Stowe's just fame ; but it cannot be reasonably denied that in her other works—notably in *Dred*, and the *Minister's Wooing*—the high-water mark of the great negro novel of *Uncle Tom* is not exactly reached.

In regard to Harriet Beecher Stowe the Rev. J. H. Twichell, in a monograph on her home life in Hartford, described her, as long ago as 1888, as being in her quiet home, attended by her daughters, surrounded by respect and affection, filled with the divine calm of Christian faith, and in perfect charity with all mankind. In that home there were many prized possessions connected with her illustrious literary past. One of these is a gold chain of just ten links, which, when Mrs. Stowe during her visit to Europe was received at Stafford House, the Duchess of Sutherland took from her own arm and clasped on that of the writer of *Uncle*

Tom's Cabin, saying : " This is the memorial of a chain which we trust will soon be broken ".

One of the best of American novelists perhaps, in the delineation without exaggeration of the trials and troubles of married life, is Amelia E. Barr, author of *A Daughter of Fife, Paul and Christina*, and of *Jan Vedder's Wife*. This last novel, indeed, is one of great interest. It opens in the Shetland Islands with the betrothal of Jan Vedder to Margaret Fae ; and the sketch given of Lerwick is equal to some of the best old Dutch paintings for its fidelity to still life, while the human element is touched in with dramatic realism. Soon after marriage come differences and doubts ; and at last things reach a climax when Jan forfeits his wife, his home, his good name, and finally loses his boat. The writer remarks here with fine covert satire, that "when a man has calamity upon calamity, the world generally concludes that he must be a very wicked man to deserve them. Perhaps the world is right ; but it is also just possible that the world, even with its six thousand years of garnered wisdom, may be wrong." Poor Jan has to go far away : he engages in the slave preventive service off the African coast, and proves himself a hero indeed ; but I must not reveal how the story is wrought out. Let it suffice to say that no adequate idea of its power and beauty, of its clear insight into human motive, and its fine analysis of human feeling, can be obtained from any skeleton outline.

Another distinguished American novelist is Louisa May Alcott, whose charming story, *Little Women*, is so widely known and universally liked. *Good Wives*, *Something to Do*, and *Fireside and Camp Stories* are among her novels. It has been truly said that Miss Alcott's fictions have imparted genuine happiness to thousands and thousands of the young, and those thrice happy elders who keep young in heart and feeling.

Another novelist of the quiet domestic type, full of thoughtful sensibility, is Miss Cummins, the author, among other works, of the *Lamplighter*, wherein we have the feat performed, and well performed too, of creating a strong human interest about a poor lamplighter in an American city. Mention must be made of another novelist, E. Wetherell (a pseudonym for Susan Warner). Her novels, the *Wide, Wide World*, and *Queechy*, have been enormously circulated, and decidedly possess charms. The character delineation is good; and if the incidents are tame and insipid to some readers, it is because such have fed intellectually too long on the hot-spiced meats, and have drank too deeply of the intoxicating and unnatural wines of the sensational writers. I have often thought that the

author of the *Wide, Wide World* is really a kind
of American Hemans in prose,—quiet, gentle, and
true, and converting the hearthstone into a very
altar of pure love and enduring faith.

Of more recent years Anna Katherine Green has
won much popularity by her highly sensational
stories, of which the *Leavenworth Case*, *A Strange
Disappearance*, and *7 to 12*, a detective story, are
good types.

Captain Mayne Reid, although entirely identified
with American fiction, was a native of Ireland, but
he may be said to have both naturalised and ac-
climatised himself as an American citizen. He had
originally a taste for travel, and early in life set out
for Mexico, and having during some years made
repeated excursions up the Red River trading and
shooting, he insensibly acquired a comprehensive
knowledge of Indian life.   He then travelled
through all the States of the Union, observing
character; and eventually, when in 1845 war broke
out between the Union and Mexico, he obtained a
commission in the American army.   He was present at the capture of Vera Cruz, and leading a
forlorn hope at Chapultepec he was seriously
wounded.   He afterwards sought to join the Hun-
garians in 1849; but could not get further than
Paris before the insurrection collapsed. Previously
Mayne Reid had written a little, but he then

settled in London and devoted himself to fiction, producing the *Rifle Rangers,* and the *Scalp Hunters,* in both of which he recounted much of his own personal experiences. Among his other novels may be mentioned the *Quadroon,* the *War Trail,* and the *Headless Horseman.* Love, war, revenge, adventure, and terrible episodes, evolved out of the convulsions of Nature, are the leading features of Mayne Reid's richly-coloured fiction. He is a strong writer, full of virility ; and although he indulges over much in pure romance, and often flies high on the wings of an exalted sentimentality, he usually relieves his impassioned passages by the introduction of amusing and humorous characters. He is a skilful painter of landscape, and has given us some lovely pictures of the prairie, which, with its innumerable flowers, he calls the " Garden of God ". He is, moreover, a manly exponent of sound morality and genuine courage, and besides his novels he has produced a multitude of really clever and exceedingly popular books for boys. No writer, perhaps, has made better use of his personal observation of the fauna and flora of strange lands ; and a good deal may be learned from his fiction of the aspects of much of the North American continent, especially in its sub-tropical regions.

Murray, the author of the *Prairie Bird,* must not

be forgotten ; nor Gustav Aimard, already alluded to, with his many stirring Indian tales.

The latter, indeed, is a writer who became Americanised like Captain Mayne Reid, and actually travelled and had real adventures in the regions of South America, whereof he writes so graphically. He has strong local colouring, and a thorough knowledge of the Indians of the South American continent. Many of his stories are anticipations of Mr. Rider Haggard, so far as the " fighting " goes ; and undoubtedly in what has been called the blood-curdling line he comes close to Cooper—Cooper as he is in such a thrilling narrative as that of the *Borderers*.

An American novelist not to be passed over is the late Dr. Oliver Wendell Holmes. He was essentially a Bostonian, and for fifty years was busy with his pen. To many he is, perhaps, best known as the *Autocrat of the Breakfast Table*, and by much charming, graceful and elegant verse. One of his most characteristic fictions is *Elsie Venner*. It is a strange product of imagination, and combines in a remarkable manner meta- physics with physiology. It is throughout an original and arrestive book, from the introduction of Wentworth Langdon, " dead-headed " into the world some fifty years ago, and who " had sat with his hands in his pockets staring at the show ever since," to the touching end of Elsie herself.

An American lady, writing of Dr. Oliver Wendell Holmes (Alice Wellington Rollins), remarks "that the genius of Holmes is well-nigh unique in the fact that dealing almost exclusively with human beings, —not merely human nature exhibited in maxims, —rarely wandering into discussions of books, or art, or landscape, it is almost entirely independent of any environment whatever. He has been anchored to one locality. . . . Once in *Elsie Venner* there is an escape like Hawthorne's into the realm of the psychological and weird . . . but the great mass of the work which has appealed to so wide a class of readers with such permanent power, appeals to them because, dealing with men and women, it deals with no particular men and women. In a word, we are reminded that, Bostonian though he be, the human beings in his stories are no more Bostonians than the ducks of his aviary are Charles River ducks . . . they are ducks, and not merely Boston ducks."

Mr. Clemens ("Mark Twain") has written much humorous fiction; one of his best efforts in serious romance, veined with all his marked peculiarities, is found in the *Prince and the Pauper*. This work is based on a daring conception. It is supposed that young Edward VI. during the life of his father desired to know something of the free life of one of his poor subjects; and in his palace exchanged apparel with a lad who, when arrayed as the prince, almost exactly resembled him. The prince on returning to the palace forgets his changed and ragged appearance, and is refused admittance. The pauper lad determines to remain master of the situation, and, as may be imagined, what ensues abounds in ingenious and surprising incidents naturally arising out of such a strange position.

Mr. E. P. Roe's novels and tales have had, I believe, a very large circulation. Many of the titles are quaint, as *He fell in Love with his own Wife*. Some others of his novels may be cited, such as *Barriers Burned Away, Driven Back to Eden, Near to Nature's Heart, A Knight of the Nineteenth Century, Miss Lou, The Earth Trembled,* and *Without a Home*.

One of the later American fictionists is Mr. Harold Frederic, the author of *In the Valley*, the *Return of the O'Mahony*, and of the *Copperhead*, or stories of the North during the American Civil War.

Among the later workers in the fields of American fiction is Mr. Henry James, who has travelled far, and now spends much time in Italy. More than twenty years ago, Mr. James began as a novelist with a work entitled *Watch and Ward*, and since then many excellent fictions have flowed from his pen. He excels mainly in drawing character and developing it through dialogue, his novels having but little of what is commonly understood as plot. Few writers, however, have so accurately delineated the American as he is when abroad, and Mr. James occupies a unique place in fiction.

It will be seen that America is already rich in fiction ; and great as has been the performance, greater far is the promise of the fiction yet to come.

INDEX.

INDEX.

AUTHORS.

TITLES.

20 *

ABERDEEN UNIVERSITY PRESS.

A FEW PRESS OPINIONS

ON

A GUIDE TO BRITISH AND AMERICAN NOVELS

Spectator.—"Mr. Russell is justified in his claim to have made a thirty-six years' study of all kinds of English fiction. His familiarity with every form of novel is amazing, and his summaries of plots and comments thereupon are as brief and lucid as they are various. The index is a careful and useful one—a guide within a guide, which will much serve the inquirer as to Mr. Russell's theories. In his study of Thackeray, Mr. Russell is careful and sympathetic."

Morning Post.—"This book is the result of much patient industry, and will be of considerable value as a Chronological Catalogue."

Globe.—"Is unquestionably useful."

Manchester Courier.—"In this book Mr. Russell has compressed much useful information on novels written in English by British, Australian, and Colonial writers. What he has to say about the great writers of the past is sound . . . an invaluable storehouse of facts."

Liverpool Post.—"Those who set themselves to assimilate the contents of the book will undoubtedly come possessed of a good general outline knowledge of the imaginative literature of British, American, and Australian fiction. The reader will find himself greatly assisted, for reference purposes, by a full index of authors and another of titles."

Leeds Mercury.—"That skilful and industrious book-maker, Mr. Percy Russell, coming forward with a book which classifies a large number of works of fiction under something like a scientific system. Mr. Russell is easily first in this sort of work. . . Mr. Russell is both intelligent and interesting, and he has worked upon a plan that seems distinctly scientific . . . Mr. Russell's book will be found uncommonly useful. Due digestion of its eighteen chapters ought to qualify a man in everything relating to fiction, British, American, and Australian."

Newcastle Weekly Chronicle.—"A large amount of information on British and American novels. He shows not only wide reading . . . thoughtful criticism. . . . This Guide may be recommended to librarians as well as to readers of fiction."

Black and White.—"Mr. Russell, already well known for his admirable 'Authors' Manual,' has here compiled a comprehensive guide to the writers of English, American, and Australian fiction. The Guide is a monument of labour carefully undertaken."

Glasgow Herald.—"Mr. Percy Russell's manual will serve a useful purpose. . . . Mr. Percy Russell has some eminently sensible remarks on the absence of cheerfulness in many modern novels."

Evening News and Post.—"As a book of reference the volume will be found useful . . . excellence of arrangement."

People.—"Pleasant and instructive. It shows a wide area of attentive reading, together with no small amount of critical faculty."

Scots Magazine.—"Will be indispensable to librarians and novel-readers generally. We cannot speak in too high terms of praise of this Guide."

Hereford Times.—"As this book is the result of thirty-six years' continuous study of British, American, and Australian fiction, we are led to expect great results, and in this Mr. Russell does not disappoint us. Mr. Russell has studied his subject with care, and the Guide supplies much useful information."

LONDON: DIGBY, LONG & CO., PUBLISHERS.

SUPPLEMENTARY LIST.

DIGBY, LONG & CO.'S
NEW NOVELS, STORIES, Etc.

IN ONE VOLUME, Price **6s.**

NEW NOVEL BY ANNIE THOMAS (Mrs PENDER CUDLIP).

False Pretences. By the Author of "Allerton Towers," "That Other Woman," "Kate Valliant," "A Girl's Folly," etc., etc. Crown 8vo, cloth, 6s.
[*Second Edition. Just out.*

The *WORLD* says:—"Miss Annie Thomas has rarely drawn a character so cleverly as that of the false and scheming Mrs Colraine."

NEW NOVEL BY DR ARABELLA KENEALY.

Some Men are such Gentlemen. By the Author of "Dr Janet of Harley Street," "Molly and Her Man-o'-War," etc. Crown 8vo, cloth, 6s. With a Frontispiece. [*Fourth Edition. Just out.*

The *ACADEMY* says:—" We take up a book by Miss Arabella Kenealy confidently expecting to be amused, and in her latest work we are not disappointed. The story is so brightly written that our interest is never allowed to flag. The heroine. Lois Clinton, is sweet and womanly. . . . The tale is told with spirit and vivacity, and shows no little skill in its descriptive passages."
The *PALL MALL GAZETTE* says:—" A book to be read breathlessly from beginning to end. It is decidedly original . . . its vivid interest. The picture of the girl is admirably drawn. The style is bright and easy."

NEW NOVEL BY DORA RUSSELL.

The Other Bond. By the Author of "A Hidden Chain," "A Country Sweetheart," etc., etc. Crown 8vo, cloth, 6s. [*Third Edition. Just out.*

The *ATHENÆUM* on Miss Russell's Works, says:—" Miss Russell writes easily and well, and she has the gift of making her characters describe themselves by their dialogue, which is bright and natural."
The *BIRMINGHAM POST* says:—" One of the best novels from the pen of Miss Dora Russell."
The *ACADEMY* says:—" Miss Dora Russell is the sole heir of Miss Braddon "

NEW NOVEL BY L. T. MEADE.

A Life for a Love. By the Author of "The Medicine Lady," "A Soldier of Fortune," "In an Iron Grip," etc., etc. Crown 8vo, cloth, 6s. With a Frontispiece by Hal Hurst. [*Third Edition. Just out.*

The *DAILY TELEGRAPH* says:—"This thrilling tale. The plot is worked out with remarkable ingenuity The book abounds in clever and graphic characterisation."
The *LIVERPOOL POST* says:—" The appetite of the reader is whetted and his curiosity excited to such a pitch that he is bound to pursue the luring tale."

18 *Bouverie Street, Fleet Street, London.*

NEW NOVELS AND STORIES—Continued.
NEW NOVEL BY FLORENCE MARRYAT.

The Beautiful Soul. By the Author of "A Fatal Silence," "There is no Death," etc., etc. Crown 8vo, cloth, 6s. *[Fourth Edition. Just out.*

The *GUARDIAN* says:—"We read the book with real pleasure and interest . . . In Felecia Hetherington, Miss Marryat has drawn a really fine character, and has given her what she claims for her in the title, a beautiful soul."
The *WORLD* says:—"An entertaining and animated story. . . . One of the most lovable women to whom novel readers have been introduced."

Une Culotte: An Impossible Story of Modern Oxford. By "TIVOLI," Author of "A Defender of the Faith." With Illustrations by A. W. COOPER. Crown 8vo, cloth, 6s. *[Second Edition.*

The *DAILY CHRONICLE* says:—"The book is full of funny things. The story is a screaming farce, and will furnish plenty of amusement."
The *MANCHESTER COURIER* says:—"A brightly-written story, of unflagging interest, dealing with the strange adventures of two audacious, but none the less charming heroines. The story is brightly told, the plot is amusing, and the characters well drawn."

The Vengeance of Medea. By EDITH GRAY WHEELWRIGHT. Crown 8vo, cloth, 6s.

The *WESTERN DAILY MERCURY* says:—"Miss Wheelwright has introduced several delightful characters, and produced a work which will add to her reputation. The dialogue is especially well written."

A Ruined Life. By EMILY ST CLAIR. Crown 8vo, cloth, 6s.

The *BIRMINGHAM GAZETTE* says:—"A powerful story developed with considerable dramatic skill and remarkable fervour."

A Dawnless Fate. By IVON HAMILTON CAMPION. Crown 8vo, cloth, 6s.

VANITY FAIR says:—"A remarkable tale, very well told."
The *LITERARY WORLD* says:—Characterised by a good deal of rugged power. The story is well conceived and worked out."

The Westovers. By ALGERNON RIDGEWAY. Author of "Westover's Ward," "Diana Fontaine," etc. Crown 8vo, cloth, 6s.

The *GLASGOW HERALD* says:—"'The Westovers' is a clever book."

The Flaming Sword. Being an Account of the Extraordinary Adventures and Discoveries of Dr PERCIVAL in the Wilds of Africa. Written by Himself. Crown 8vo, cloth, 6s.

The *SPEAKER* says:—"Mr Rider Haggard himself has not imagined more wonderful things than those which befell Dr Percival and his friends."
The *LITERARY WORLD* says:—"Out-Haggards Haggard."

In Due Season. By AGNES GOLDWIN. Crown 8vo, cloth, 6s.

The *ACADEMY* says:—"Her novel is well written, it flows easily, its situations are natural, its men and women are real"

NEW NOVELS AND STORIES—*Continued.*

His Last Amour. By MONOPOLE. Crown 8vo, cloth, 6s.

The *GLASGOW HERALD* says:—"The story is unfolded with considerable skill, and the interest of the reader is not allowed to flag."

The *COURT CIRCULAR* says:—" From first to last the interest of the reader is sustained in this powerfully written book."

An Unknown Power. By CHARLES E. R. BELLAIRS Crown 8vo, cloth, 6s.

The *BELFAST NORTHERN WHIG* says:—"From start to finish the reader's attention is never allowed to flag. The characters are drawn with con siderable fidelity to life. The plot is original, and its developments well worked out."

NEW NOVEL BY GERTRUDE L. WARREN.

The Mystery of Hazelgrove. By GERTRUDE L. WARREN. Crown 8vo, cloth, 6s.   [*Just out.*

NEW NOVEL BY DR ARABELLA KENEALY.

The Honourable Mrs Spoor. By the Author of "Some Men are such Gentlemen," "Dr Janet of Harley Street," etc. Crown 8vo, cloth, 6s.

[*In May.*

NEW NOVEL BY ALICE MAUD MEADOWS.

When the Heart is Young. By the Author of "The Romance of a Madhouse," etc. Crown 8vo, cloth. 6s.   [*Second Edition. Just out.*

IN THREE VOLUMES, Price **31s. 6d.**

BY DORA RUSSELL.

A Hidden Chain. By the Author of "Footprints in the Snow," "The Other Bond," etc., etc. In Three Volumes, crown 8vo, cloth, 31s. 6d. [*Second Edition.*

BY JEAN MIDDLEMASS.

The Mystery of Clement Dunraven. By the Author of "A Girl in a Thousand," etc. In Three Volumes, crown 8vo, cloth, 31s. 6d. [*Second Edition.*

BY PERCY ROSS.

The Eccentrics. By the Author of "A Comedy without Laughter," "A Misguidit Lassie," "A Professor of Alchemy," etc. In Three Volumes, crown 8vo, cloth, 31s. 6d.

BY GILBERTA M. F. LYON.

Absent Yet Present. By the Author of "For Good or Evil." In Three Volumes, crown 8vo, cloth, 31s. 6d.

BY MADELINE CRICHTON.

Like a Sister. In Three Volumes, crown 8vo, cloth, 31s. 6d.   [*Second Edition.*

NEW NOVELS AND STORIES—*Continued.*
IN ONE VOLUME, Price **3s. 6d.**

NEW BOOK BY THE AUTHOR OF "A PLUNGE INTO SPACE."

The Crack of Doom. By ROBERT CROMIE, Author of "For England's Sake," etc. Crown 8vo, cloth, 3s. 6d. *[Immediately.*

Her Loving Slave. By HUME NISBET, author of "The Jolly Roger," "Bail Up," etc., etc. In Handsome Pictorial Binding, with Illustrations by the Author. Crown 8vo, cloth, 3s. 6d. *[Third Edition.*

The *TIMES* says:—" Has abundance of go in it.
The *STANDARD* says :—" It is a good story well told."
The *ST JAMES'S BUDGET* says:—"The whole story is capitally written, the characters are life-like, and the whole is in Mr Nisbet's best style."

His Egyptian Wife. By HILTON HILL. Crown 8vo, cloth, 3s. 6d. With Frontispiece. Published this day simultaneously in London and New York.

A Son of Noah. By MARY ANDERSON. Crown 8vo, cloth, 3s. 6d. (FIFTH EDITION.)

The Last Cruise of the Teal. By LEIGH RAY. In handsome pictorial binding. Illustrated through-out. Crown 8vo, cloth, 3s. 6d. (SECOND EDITION.)

The *NATIONAL OBSERVER* says :—" It is long since we have lighted on so good a story of adventure."

His Troublesome Sister. By EVA TRAVERS EVERED POOLE, Author of many Popular Stories. Crown 8vo, cloth, 3s. 6d.

The *BIRMINGHAM POST* says:—"An interesting and well-constructed story. The characters are strongly drawn, the plot is well devised, and those who commence the book will be sure to finish it."

The Bow and the Sword. A Romance. By E. C. ADAMS, M.A. With 16 full-page drawings by MATTHEW STRETCH. Crown 8vo, pictorial cloth, 3s. 6d.

The *MORNING POST* says:—" The author reconstructs cleverly the life of one of the most cultivated nations of antiquity, and describes both wars and pageants with picturesque vigour. The illustrations are well executed."

The Maid of Havodwen. By JOHN FERRARS. Author of "Claud Brennan." Crown 8vo, cloth, 3s. 6d.

The *DUNDEE ADVERTISER* says :—" A charming story of Welsh life and character. . . . Deeply interesting. . . . Of unusual attractiveness."

Paths that Cross. By MARK TREHERN. Crown 8vo, cloth, 3s. 6d.

The *DAILY TELEGRAPH* says:—" Cleverly sketched characters. The book is enlivened throughout with innumerable light touches of quaint and spontaneous humour."

A Tale of Two Curates. By Rev. JAMES COPNER, M.A. Crown 8vo, cloth, 3s. 6d.

The *DUNDEE ADVERTISER* says:—" Simply but graphically narrated."

NEW NOVELS AND STORIES—*Continued.*

The Wrong of Fate. By LILLIAS LOBENHOFFER, Author of "Bairnie," etc. Crown 8vo, cloth, 3s. 6d.

The *LONDON STAR* says:—"A well-written and clever novel. excellent studies of Scotch character."
The *SCOTSMAN* says:—"Shows considerable power."

Studies in Miniature. By A TITULAR VICAR. Crown 8vo, cloth, 3s. 6d.

The *MANCHESTER COURIER* says:—"Brightly and cleverly written."
The *BELFAST NEWS LETTER* says:—"Very readable, characters admirably drawn."

Spunyarn. By N. J. PRESTON. Crown 8vo, pictorial cloth, 3s. 6d.   [*Just out.*

IN ONE VOLUME, Price **2s. 6d.**

Lost! £100 Reward. By MIRIAM YOUNG, Author of "The Girl Musician." Crown 8vo, cloth, 2s. 6d.

The *WEEKLY SUN* says:—"The interest is well sustained throughout, and the incidents are most graphically described."

Clenched Antagonisms. By LEWIS IRAM. Crown 8vo, cloth, 2s. 6d.

The *SATURDAY REVIEW* says:—"'Clenched Antagonisms' is a powerful and ghastly narrative of the triumph of force over virtue. The book gives a striking illustration of the barbarous incongruities that still exist in the midst of an advanced civilisation."

My Village. By R. MENZIES FERGUSSON, M.A., Author of "Our Trip North," etc., etc. Crown 8vo, pictorial cloth, 2s. 6d.

The *LITERARY WORLD* says:—"This is an interesting book. The scenes depicted will revive in many breasts enchanting memories of bygone years, and obscure villages far away."

For Marjory's Sake: A Story of South Australian Country Life. By Mrs JOHN WATERHOUSE. In handsome cloth binding, with Illustrations. Crown 8vo, cloth, 2s. 6d.

The *LITERARY WORLD* says:—"A delightful little volume, fresh and dainty, and with the pure, free air of Australian country parts blowing through it . . . gracefully told . . . the writing is graceful and easy."

IN ONE VOLUME, PAPER COVER, Price **1s.**

A Stock Exchange Romance. By BRACEBRIDGE HEMYNG, Author of "The Stockbroker's Wife," "Called to the Bar," etc., etc. Edited by GEORGE GREGORY. Crown 8vo, picture cover, 1s. (TENTH THOUSAND.)

Our Discordant Life. By ADAM D'HÉRISTAL. Crown 8vo, picture cover, 1s.

A Police Sergeant's Secret. By KILSYTH STELLIER, Author of "Taken by Force." Crown 8vo, picture cover, 1s. (FIFTH THOUSAND.)

Irish Stew. By JAMES J. MORAN, Author of "A Deformed Idol," "The Dunferry Risin'," "Runs in the Blood," etc. Crown 8vo, lithographed cover, price 1s. *[Just out.*

The *WEEKLY SUN* says :—" Mr MORAN is the 'Barrie ' of Ireland. . . . In a remote district in the west of Ireland he has created an Irish Thrums."

DIGBY'S POPULAR NOVEL SERIES.

In Handsome Cloth Binding, Gold Lettered, Cr. 8vo, 320 pp. Price **2s. 6d.** *each, or in Picture Boards, Price* **2s.** *each.*

BY JEAN MIDDLEMASS.

THE MYSTERY OF CLEM-ENT DUNRAVEN. By the Author of "A Girl in a Thousand," etc. (SECOND EDITION.)

BY DR. A. KENEALY.

Dr JANET OF HARLEY STREET. By the Author of "Molly and her Man-o'-War," etc. (SEVENTH EDITION.) With Portrait.

BY DORA RUSSELL.

A HIDDEN CHAIN. By the Author of "Footprints in the Snow," etc. (SECOND EDITION.)

BY HUME NISBET.

THE JOLLY ROGER. By the Author of "Bail Up," etc. With Illustrations by the Author. (FIFTH EDITION.)

NOTE.—Other Works in the same Series in due course.

MISCELLANEOUS.

A History of the Great Western Railway from Its Inception to the Present Time. By G. A. SEKON. Revised by F. G. SAUNDERS, Chairman of the Great Western Railway. Demy 8vo, 390 pages, cloth, 7s. 6d. With numerous Illustrations.

** *Illustrated Prospectus, post free.* [*Second Edition.*

The *TIMES*, April 12th, 1895.—" Mr Sekon's volume is full of interest, and constitutes an important chapter in the history of railway development in England."

The *STANDARD* (Leader), April 4th, 1895.—" An excellent addition to the literature of our iron roads."

The *DAILY TELEGRAPH*. April 13th, 1895.—" Mr G. A. Sekon has performed a service to the public. His book is full of interest, and is evidently the result of a great deal of painstaking inquiry. . . . His book is made all the more valuable by several pictures of engines, collisions, the Saltash Bridge, the Old Bath Station and the Box Tunnel ; and it will be welcomed by all interested in the history and extraordinary expansion of our iron roadways "

MISCELLANEOUS—*Continued.*

The Autobiography of an Old Passport, 1839-1889,
chiefly relating how we accomplished many Driving Tours with our own English Horses over the Roads of Western Europe before the time of Railways. By the Rev. ALFRED CHARLES SMITH, M.A., Author of "Attractions of the Nile," "A Spring Tour in Portugal," "A Pilgrimage through Palestine," etc. With numerous illustrations. Royal 8vo, cloth extra, 21s.

The *DAILY NEWS* says:—" There is a refreshing flavour in these chatty Diaries . . . these lively and amusing reminiscences. . . . There is nothing in the tours and trips of to-day to compare with them in charm."

Three Empresses.
Josephine, Marie-Louise, Eugénie. By CAROLINE GEAREY, Author of "In Other Lands," etc. With portraits. Cr. 8vo, cloth, 6s. (SECOND EDIT.)

The *PALL MALL GAZETTE* says:—" This charming book. . . Gracefully and graphically written, the story of each Empress is clearly and fully told. . . . This delightful book."

Winter and Summer Excursions in Canada.
. By C. L. JOHNSTONE, Author of "Historical Families of Dumfriesshire," etc. With Illustrations. Crown 8vo, cloth, 6s.

The *DAILY NEWS* says:—" Not for a long while have we read a book of its class which deserves so much confidence. Intending settlers would do well to study Mr Johnstone's book."

The Author's Manual.
By PERCY RUSSELL. With Prefatory Remarks by Mr GLADSTONE. Crown 8vo, cloth, 3s. 6d. net. (EIGHTH AND CHEAPER EDITION.) With portrait.

The *WESTMINSTER REVIEW* says:—". . Mr Russell's book is a very complete manual and guide for journalist and author. It is not a merely practical work—it is literary and appreciative of literature in its best sense: . . . we have little else but praise for the volume."

A Guide to British and American Novels.
From the Earliest Period to the end of 1894. By PERCY RUSSELL, Author of "The Author's Manual," etc. Crown 8vo, cloth. Price 3s. 6d. net. (SECOND EDITION CAREFULLY REVISED.)

The *SPECTATOR* says:—" Mr Russell's familiarity with every form of novel is amazing, and his summaries of plots and comments thereon are as brief and lucid as they are various."
GLOBE says:—" Is unquestionably useful."
MORNING POST says :—" Will be of considerable value."
MANCHESTER COURIER says:—" An invaluable storehouse of facts."
NEWCASTLE CHRONICLE says:—" The Guide may be recommended to librarians as well as to readers of fiction."

MISCELLANEOUS—*Continued.*

Sixty Years' Experience as an Irish Landlord.

Memoirs of John Hamilton, D.L. of St Ernan's, Donegal. Edited, with Introduction, by the Rev. H C. White, late Chaplain, Paris. Crown 8vo, cloth, 6s. With Portrait.

The *TIMES* says:—"Much valuable light on the real history of Ireland, and of the Irish agrarian question in the present century is thrown by a very interesting volume entitled 'Sixty Years' Experience as an Irish Landlord.' . . . This very instructive volume."

Nigh on Sixty Years at Sea. By Robert Wool

ward ("Old Woolward"). Crown 8vo, cloth, 6s. With Portrait. (Second Edition.)

The *TIMES* says:—"Very entertaining reading. Captain Woolward writes sensibly and straightforwardly, and tells his story with the frankness of an old salt. He has a keen sense of humour, and his stories are endless and very entertaining."

Whose Fault? The Story of a Trial at *Nisi Prius.*

By Ellis J. Davis, Barrister-at-Law. In handsome pictorial binding. Crown 8vo, cloth, 3s. 6d.

The *TIMES* says:—"An ingenious attempt to convey to the lay mind an accurate and complete idea of the origin and progress and all the essential circumstances of an ordinary action at law. The idea is certainly a good one, and is executed in very entertaining fashion. . . . Mr Davis's instructive little book."

Borodin and Liszt. I.—Life and Works of a Russian

Composer. II.—Liszt, as sketched in the Letters of Borodin. By Alfred Habets. Translated with a Preface by Rosa Newmarch. With Portraits and Fac-similes. [*Immediately.*

Fragments from Victor Hugo's Legends and Lyrics. By Cecilia Elizabeth Meetkerke.

Crown 8vo, cloth, 7s. 6d.

The *WORLD* says:—"The most admirable rendering of French poetry into English that has come to our knowledge since Father Prout's translation of 'La Chant du Cosaque.'"

BY THE AUTHOR OF "SONG FAVOURS."

Minutiæ. By Charles William Dalmon. Royal 16mo, cloth elegant, price 2s. 6d.

The *ACADEMY* says:—"His song has a rare and sweet note. The little book has colour and fragrance, and is none the less welcome because the fragrance is delicate, evanescent; the colours of white and silver grey and lavender, rather than brilliant and exuberant. . . . Mr Dalmon's genuine artistry. In his sonnets he shows a deft touch, particularly in the fine one, 'Ecce Ancilla Domini.' Yet. after all, it is in the lyrics that he is most individual. . Let him take heart, for surely the song that he has to sing is worth singing."

** A complete Catalogue of Novels, Travels, Biographies, Poems, etc., with a critical or descriptive notice of each, free by post on application.

London: DIGBY, LONG & CO., Publishers,
18 *Bouverie Street, Fleet Street, E.C.*

www.ingramcontent.com/pod-product-compliance
Lightning Source LLC
Chambersburg PA
CBHW022248020726
47496CB00004B/1120